Experience Design
A Framework for
Integrating Brand,
Experience, and Value

WITHDRAWN FROM
THE LIBRARY

KA 0384165 0

Experience Design
A Framework for
Integrating Brand,
Experience, and Value

Patrick Newbery
Kevin Farnham

UNIVERSITY OF WINCHESTER
LIBRARY

Cover image and design: Method, Inc.

This book is printed on acid-free paper.

Copyright © 2013 by Patrick Newbery, Kevin Farnham, and Method, Inc. All rights reserved.

Published by John Wiley & Sons, Inc., Hoboken, New Jersey.
Published simultaneously in Canada.

No part of this publication may be reproduced, stored in a retrieval system, or transmitted in any form or by any means, electronic, mechanical, photocopying, recording, scanning, or otherwise, except as permitted under Section 107 or 108 of the 1976 United States Copyright Act, without either the prior written permission of the Publisher, or authorization through payment of the appropriate per-copy fee to the Copyright Clearance Center, 222 Rosewood Drive, Danvers, MA 01923, (978) 750-8400, fax (978) 646-8600, or on the web at www.copyright .com. Requests to the Publisher for permission should be addressed to the Permissions Department, John Wiley & Sons, Inc., 111 River Street, Hoboken, NJ 07030, (201) 748-6011, fax (201) 748-6008, or online at www.wiley .com/go/permissions.

While the publisher and author have used their best efforts in preparing this book, they make no representations or warranties with respect to the accuracy or completeness of the contents of this book and specifically disclaim any implied warranties of merchantability or fitness for a particular purpose. No warranty may be created or extended by sales representatives or written sales materials. The advice and strategies contained herein may not be suitable for your situation. You should consult with a professional where appropriate. Neither the publisher nor the author shall be liable for damages arising herefrom.

For general information about our other products and services, please contact our Customer Care Department within the United States at (800) 762-2974, outside the United States at (317) 572-3993 or fax (317) 572-4002.

Wiley publishes in a variety of print and electronic formats and by print-on-demand. Some material included with standard print versions of this book may not be included in e-books or in print-on-demand. If this book refers to media such as a CD or DVD that is not included in the version you purchased, you may download this material at http://booksupport.wiley.com. For more information about Wiley products, visit www.wiley.com.

Library of Congress Cataloging-in-Publication Data:

Newbery, Patrick
Experience Design : A Framework for Integrating Brand, Experience, and Value
/ Patrick Newbery and Kevin Farnham.
p. cm
  Includes index.
ISBN 978-1-118-60963-7 (paper); ISBN 978-1-118-72856-7 (ebk); ISBN 978-1-118-72839-0 (ebk); ISBN 978-1-118-72838-3 (ebk)
1. Product design. 2. Industrial design. I. Farnham, Kevin. Title.
TS171.F37 2013
658.5'752—dc23   2013014154

Printed in the United States of America

10 9 8 7 6 5 4 3 2 1

UNIVERSITY OF WINCHESTER

Contents

Introduction

There have been incredible changes in the business landscape over the past few decades. Technology and globalization have made it possible to see the entire world as a market that is always on. Industries that have been rock solid find that their foundations are rapidly eroding, and new start-ups are given valuations in the millions without having a proven revenue model. The options available to consumers are rapidly expanding, and at the same time, consolidation is the strategy chosen by some businesses to ensure that they can continue to meet consumer demand and provide returns for shareholders.

All of this raises the question: How does anyone stay in business? How do you stay in business? Or perhaps the more appropriate question for the majority of us is: How does the company we work for stay in business? Most of us engage in a process that creates value for someone else—our customers. We create enough value that they are willing to pay money in exchange for it. And we stay in business by charging more for this value than it costs us to create it.

Value is predicated on asymmetry. *The Merriam-Webster Dictionary* defines *value* as "a fair return or equivalent in goods, services, or money for something exchanged." Inherent in this definition is that one side has something that the other desires. This is the basic asymmetry. But in many cases, there is an underlying asymmetry in information. Someone knows how to make something that another doesn't; someone has used knowledge to produce a good or service that another person needs but doesn't have the requisite knowledge (or resources at hand) to produce on his or her own.

The basic purpose of business is conducting a value exchange with the ability to achieve a financial benefit. Businesses exist when they can (profitably) create value for customers. This value comes in different flavors. The reason for this differential is that different products and services can fill different needs. Tangible value is relatively easy to demonstrate and quantify; it is objective. It appeals to a broad number of people who have a similar need and would all agree on how it should be met. This is a basic aspect of almost every product or service. Often, the scarcity of products delivering only tangible value, as well as the immediacy or importance of the need they fulfill, determine how much demand and what kind of pricing they can command. Most basic products and commodities fall into this category.

There is also intangible value, which can be harder to demonstrate, and is best described through qualities. Whether or not a person agrees there is value in it tends to be more subjective. Many products or services imply some aspect of intangible value. In some cases, the intangible value is based on aggregation of specialized tangible value, where the excess is not needed by all but is nice for some people to have for practical needs (professional-level tools). In this case where the buyer of this kind of value may never actually need to use it, the value is really measured in how possessing this excess of tangible value fulfills an emotional or psychological need of the buyer: security, excitement, habit, and so forth. Because it is intangible and subjective, this kind of value is often only truly measurable by the individual. Many nonessential products and services or things that command a premium fall into this category. And many products or services compete based on how their intangible value differentiates them from others.

Finally, there is aspirational value, which is related to intangible value but with a slight twist. Here, rather than merely satisfying an internally defined need, aspirational value is often tied to the status and desires of an individual person; things we want to believe about ourselves, or things we want others to believe about us. In other words, it is about satisfying an internal need in an outward way. Aspirational value is often an attribute of luxury products and services and is commonly the underlying premise of brands (brand being a belief system originally developed to differentiate one's products from those of competitors when relying on tangible value would be insufficient).

Today's intricate businesses, industries, and economies are built on chains and networks of value creation. These can be quite complex—multitiered, vertically integrated, and synergistically aligned. The result of this happening at a global level is that there are fewer and fewer things one can make or obtain for oneself that are of lesser cost and better quality than one can buy from someone else. In other words, consumers generally need to rely on someone else to provide many of the necessities and niceties of living.

However, one of the possibilities arising from creating and competing on intangible and aspirational value is a disparity between what value is offered and what value is received. Although this is true for tangible value as well, it's a little easier to spot the discrepancy before committing to the purchase. It's not difficult to see that the more intangible and aspirational value is involved, the more subjective this evaluation can be. Many products and services today use a hybrid of value types in communicating with markets, and much of the competition between similar offerings is driven by trying to find the right combination of value types. Add to this that value chains and networks often require many stages of effort and multiple partners to deliver value to an end customer, and determining what portion of the overall value they deliver becomes murky. It's often easier to describe what value should be there and why than it is for the customer to actually find and experience that value.

Business managers and their consultants spend a lot of time and effort looking at how to minimize the costs and optimize the processes of creating and delivering value, especially as public, political, national, and environmental constraints are taken into account. And many businesses have adroitly understood that there should also be a focus on how the customer accesses, receives, and evaluates the value their businesses provide. They spend quite a bit of time and money with consultants to figure out how best to communicate their proposed value and to whom they should be communicating.

So a modern business has many moving parts. But from a customer's perspective, what they see are facets of a single thing—an interface that connects them to the business. All the products, services, mailers, ads, customer support calls, and conversations with sales associates are part of the interface through which value is represented and ostensibly flows. And lucky enough for us (the authors), business relies on design to help create these interfaces.

How Business Uses Design to Create Value

Design has been a practice of the human mind since we first started making tools. The value of design probably didn't play much of a role in early economic transactions, which were likely just trading tools for something of more immediate value: food. Over time, design has surfaced as the foundation of many areas of skill that create our modern world. But our belief is that at some point in the evolution of the processes defining and planning for value creation and delivery, design and business aspects became separated and design took a backseat.

Perhaps part of this has to do with the duality of the word *design* itself. *Design* is both a noun and a verb. As a noun, it's the idea, artifact, and outcome of a process. As a verb, it's the process of conceiving, planning, and executing an idea. We associate this dual meaning mostly with the artifacts that are designed—cars, clothes, books, consumer electronics, houses, aircraft, and so on. Most anything human-made has benefited from the design process on its way to becoming real. We believe that the process of design has a high degree of influence on the outcome: Designing aircraft is different from designing clothes. When people who are not familiar or concerned with the process of designing a specific kind of product or service make decisions about that process (whom to work with, what they should produce, how it should be produced, how trade-offs in cost and effort affect final products, etc.), the value of the final design can be easily compromised. Sometimes the customer is the first to feel the impact of these compromises, and the experiences that this creates can be harmful to the long-term health of the business that provided the product.

Business relies on design. In creating, marketing, and delivering value, design is used to make sure that the end result is what business believes will be effective enough to connect with customers and help them realize the value they are seeking. There are as many kinds of design processes as there are design outputs. But with the focus on the final product, business can be tempted to look for the designers whose portfolios best meet what the business is attempting to do. This can lead to a cherry-picking of design skills that are better at providing a level of style or artifice, as opposed to having a deep knowledge of the process. The trade-off is that the compromises made to the process affect the outcome in ways that are not obvious to business or design but that become all too obvious to customers, much to their dissatisfaction and disappointment.

What's Changing in the Relationship and Why

This relationship between business and design has been great for the design professions. As the interface between businesses and customers takes on new forms, and occurs across new touch points, there are more opportunities for design to play a role in looking at what can be improved. New branches of design can split off from traditional practices. This creates an interesting situation. Business may increase its reliance on design to get things done, but the design processes and the resulting outcomes are harder to coordinate, now operating in parallel, across many aspects of the customer interface.

The result is that businesses spend a lot of money on design services. In many cases, they create permanent in-house design teams responsible for capital-intensive or highly proprietary value creation (where risks, such as security, need to be managed). These internal efforts often operate somewhat independently from external design processes, and are focused in different areas. Some of these internal costs are treated, at least philosophically, as investments, whereas others are viewed as expenses with no measurable return. It is up to business managers to make sure that all of these design services and the outputs they provide are coordinated with regard to creating and delivering value.

On the surface, this makes a lot of sense and allows for a degree of specialization in the design field. Theoretically, everyone is happy. But we believe that this leads to an unintended problem. If business is able to decide what and where design adds value, what is the process to make sure that the total of value and effort, as seen by the most important party—the customer (the final arbiter of value)—is greater than the sum of the parts? Or more important, what is the process to ensure that the individual design outcomes don't conflict with or create problems for each other, leading to an overall outcome that is not even equal to the sum of the parts? If the business managers don't understand the nuances of value or the design process and its effects on the design output, what's to prevent decisions that shortchange the value that design can create? And who identifies when the trade-offs are helpful or harmful and from what vantage point?

With all this to consider, business may inadvertently be asking design to create the most effective interface between itself and its customers—but in a way that actually makes it more challenging for customers. If the efficiency of this interface is key to the health and well-being of the business, then things get even more challenging for business. Of course, the challenges increase with external pressures as well.

Technology's rapid rate of change provides new problems and opportunities for creating, marketing, and delivering value. The economics of business models can be irreversibly shifted, and what was once a great business can become impossible to sustain. New forms of value can be created, and it's unclear which ones will be successful and which ones are simply novelties with no long-term viability. Some can be very compelling for customers, such as those offered at no cost (or, more accurately, no cost for now). So it's important not only to create, market, and deliver value but also to keep your customers engaged enough that they look to you, rather than a competitor, for value when they need it. (This also means you need to anticipate customers' needs and desires since if you can't provide for them, they will turn to a competitor.) Add more feedback loops to the system, and small mistakes can become amplified very quickly. In one sense, business now must outpace competitors, as well as technology itself.

If it takes more time and attention to understand where technology is taking business and business is not getting the full benefits of design (for example, by creating the right interface to deliver value to customers in a sustainable way that is also capable of growth), then what? Does it make more sense to pull design more tightly into the business? And if design is a horizontal business function, what is the mechanism for ensuring that design within different areas of the business is well orchestrated and that the benefit is greater than the sum of the efforts? What happens when design needs outstrip capacity and you need to outsource some aspects of design, as is the case in almost every company that has a healthy internal design practice and culture? We believe that the answers come from rethinking how business and design work together.

Born from Our Experience

In 1999, we launched a business, Method, Inc., offering design services to help bridge the gap between the process and outcome sides and create more value for our clients. It was our belief that businesses were buying design services based on the outcome they needed (a logo, a brochure, a website, etc.) and then looking for design studios that specialized in producing that kind of output. We believed that businesses should understand that their brands needed to be coherent across all channels and media; otherwise, they ran the risk of diluting the power of their brands. We didn't see a lot of design companies espousing this view at the time, and we believed that this approach would provide more value to our customers and, by extension, their customers.

(Full disclosure: Although the main theme of this book revolves around design, neither of us consider ourselves *practicing designers* in the conventional sense. We both found an appreciation for design, as process and outcome, and even worked as designers. But in the world of design, your success is often largely defined by your output and how celebrated the outcome is. We quickly learned that although we had an affinity for the profession, we excelled more in the process and thinking side and met lots of very talented people who excelled in the outcome side. We also saw that when those two sides of the design mind worked together, a very different kind of outcome was produced—one that was just as good from a quality standpoint, but even better at solving a problem more effectively.)

One of our first projects involved developing an identity mark (logo) for an Internet start-up. We presented three rounds of design, and the chief executive officer (CEO) of the client company didn't approve any. We spoke with our creative director and cofounder, Mike Abbink, about how the project was going.

According to Abbink, the CEO had initially chosen a direction but, upon seeing it with requested revisions, changed his mind and decided to choose another option—with minor revisions, of course. It happened again with the second choice, on the way to yet another option. It was clear to both of us that the CEO was choosing subjectively and did not have the same understanding of the process or what the real function of a visual identity mark was in building a brand. This was not an uncommon problem. We had seen it while working at other studios and decided to try a different approach. We began to co-create a set of shared business-design criteria with the our clients, before any identity work even started. We then used it in our design approach and whenever we spoke about design with the clients. We were equipping them with the criteria that could help them make a choice. After this change, our clients began choosing the final identity mark from our first-round design presentations all the time.

The takeaway for us was simple. Design and business needed more effective frameworks for sharing, thinking, and addressing needs in order to increase the effectiveness of collaboration.

Around 2007, the concept of brand experience was beginning to gain attention on both the business and design sides of the table. The premise was that broadcasting a message of what a brand stood for and expecting people to take it at face value was the wrong approach. The thinking was that there were multiple touch points that delivered brand message and value, and many of these were shifting from one-way communications controlled by the brand owner to many multidirectional communications controlled by the market.

The common view was that businesses had to better understand the values and perspectives of the customer. Instead of telling customers how to perceive a brand, it was about figuring out where the brand fit in their world and giving them a view into how it should fit. This was about understanding the customer's journey, but it was still focused on the upstream portion of product: marketing and sales.

During this emergence of the importance of brand experience, we began to observe that more and more of our clients were engaging us to develop services, as well as products. And many of these services were delivered through a new generation of networked devices. What was missing from the brand experience equation was that value delivered by a service is different from that delivered by a product. A service requires ongoing perception of value by the customer, or the customer stops paying for it, unlike a product, which is purchased once. And these services that were delivered across devices had to ensure that there was parity of value across the devices. Each device was essentially becoming a service channel, in addition to being a product in its own right.

Brand experience was more concerned about the consistency and coherency of the brand and providing an authentic connection with the market. But what was happening after the sale was made? How was a business ensuring that the myriad of points within their value interface were working in their favor?

Working with Robert Murdock, our chief creative officer at that time, we began to look at how product and service design needed to address the entire customer life cycle, rather than focusing only on tactics for winning a sale. More important, we had to find ways to keep customers engaged and to grow the relationship. We were seeing this very problem play out in ways that linked innovative consumer electronics, conventional media services, and start-ups. It was clear that this same problem was moving through every industry.

In 2009, we began sharing our perspectives about our learnings through a series of white papers and salons that we called Method 10×10 (not exactly original but adequate in that we did it to celebrate our tenth anniversary and we originally set out to do just 10 papers). One of the later papers in this series raised the question: Who in today's modern enterprise is really responsible for managing the customer experience? The title of chief experience officer is relatively new and certainly not ubiquitous. It raised the question: What systems and processes do they manage and by what criteria? And if the answer is through top-down mandate, one has to wonder how effective a top-down mandate will be in today's complex, ever-changing business environment.

Our Views on Experience Design and This Book

We believe that the requirements facing businesses today and the role that design can play in helping them meet those requirements are different from the past. We believe that a change in how business and design collaborate will come through a combination of top-down and bottom-up efforts. But to be most effective, there will need to be some common understanding and shared perspectives so that those who are closest to the change can help it thrive. For this to happen, there needs to be some kind of a framework that allows business and design to more comfortably achieve goals and share processes that make it easier for either business or design to implement.

We have therefore decided to share our experiences and thinking in order to advance the conversation and propose a new way to look at the intersection of business and design.

What We Mean by Experience Design

This book is primarily about looking at value through a new lens. We believe that looking through this lens will become increasingly relevant in the future. And although not all businesses have had to use it at all levels of their enterprises, we believe it should now be part of every business practitioner's tool kit. This lens is experience design.

Basic Overview

What do we mean by the concept of experience design? Experience design is taking a more systematic approach to how design and business look at opportunities, frame problems and projects, and evaluate solutions. The goal of this approach is to ensure that customers are receiving and recognizing the maximum value in a way that also keeps them engaged with the business.

Experience design naturally assumes it makes sense to provide adequate levels of quality in customer service at all stages of a customer relationship. But it goes beyond simply planning for adequate and encourages thinking about delivering value and growing engagement. Experience design's range does not stop at the activities in a specific channel or pertain only to things directly in the business's control. In fact, experience design should help customers get more value from the products and services they buy, not just by improving usability, but by unlocking options and potential.

How It Can Be a More Effective Approach

A fundamental aspect of experience design is realizing that experiences are tied to the passage of time: How we interpret what is happening at a particular time, what it means, how we feel about it, and what the meaning implies in regard to our future actions form our experiences. It's easy to assume that anyone developing or designing a process is thinking through the lens of time, and to some degree, this is true. But a key question is, How thoroughly are they using time as a context, and what are they doing with it? And most important, how are time and value related?

We continually see both business thinkers and designers choosing the wrong frame for using and evaluating time. Most often, time is considered from a very local and short-term perspective, for example, looking at the flow of interaction between different steps of a service or envisioning what a customer's first-time use is going to be like. They rarely think about whether the choices they make still make sense when the customer is using the product or service for the 50th time, 100th time, or even last time. Business thinkers and designers usually consider the minor problems a user may have, but not the major problems. They look at what the marketing campaign needs to say, but they don't necessarily connect it to what goes on when the user first opens the box upon returning home or uses the service for the first time. The proper consideration of time is often precluded by the predefined project scope, and the collective inexperience of the designer and client. The result may be that the project fails to meet its objectives, or worse, that the problems are never addressed, and remain unseen until they are experienced by a customer. When important options are ignored, short- and long-term goals can become disconnected.

Connecting value identification, creation, delivery, and support from brand through to product/service offerings across the entire lifetime of the customer relationship requires thinking about the relationship of time and value. The objective is to build an understanding of how to look at opportunities, issues, strategies, and tactics. And that's precisely what we believe experience design can help business and design achieve.

What This Book Isn't

The key to higher levels of customer engagement is through experiences that deliver value and provide a reason and a means for further engagement. But this book is not a checklist of tactics to improve key performance indicators or empirically measured ways to improve engagement at collaborative touch points with designers. "Why not?" you may ask. "That would be incredibly valuable!" We agree. We believe that this is a constantly moving target, and any such list would quickly become out of date. We also believe that many of these kinds of tactics become more self-evident when you view options and requirements through an experience design lens.

FYI: We have chosen not to base everything in this book on case studies. We will cite examples that we think are important in terms of explaining a point, but using case studies to prove a point can be problematic. On one hand, it would be easy to cherry-pick the case studies that support a point and ignore those that challenge it. And in many cases, the relevance or validity of a case study can change over time; what seemed like a brilliant decision and a success story at one point might prove to have been a wrong move in retrospect, despite the sound logic, clear foresight, and suitability of the choices made at the time. If you think that a business book needs real case studies to be valid, consider the fact that several very famous business books are alleged to be based on fictitious case studies or fabricated data.

This book is not a catalog of design techniques that generate an emotional response. There are times when using such techniques is very smart, and it is quite challenging and interesting to keep identifying new ways to do this. But we believe that if there isn't sufficient value to begin with, these techniques by themselves do not create long-term engagement. In fact, they may actually shorten engagement as they become expected and are seen as affectations, distractions, or wastes of time. Many designers and buyers of design services look at these techniques as being what experience design is all about, but we strongly suggest that this is a myopic view and that approaches that target emotional responses be used to increase real value, not as a substitute for it.

What This Book Is

We hope that anyone who finds this book reads it in its entirety with the aim of understanding a view of how business and design can be more successful working together. We also hope that the basic thesis provides an interesting view that can be adopted, adapted, and made better. We don't propose that this is the thing that has to happen or your business is doomed. Nor is it the definitive way to think about experience design. We simply hope that what we are putting forth here provides some insight that is useful for others, even as a reference tool. To that end, we have tried to write it in such a way that allows people to jump in and out of sections that seem most relevant to their needs.

The book is divided into three sections. The first section is intended to set the context for why experience design makes sense when looking at the intersection of business and design. Chapter 1 looks at how the role and purpose of design have been evolving over the past century or so, specifically how and why the requirements and opportunities for design to help business have been changing. Chapter 2 looks at how the notion of value, through products and services, has been changing and what this means for businesses as they think about how to better engage customers. Chapter 3 explores what is changing for business and how business's initial reaction to chase innovation is only a partial solution. The fourth and final chapter of this section presents experience design as a concept and explains the basic principles involved in thinking about things from this perspective. It is our hope that by providing a background to the concept of experience design, we will help readers better consider the need for and potential benefits of the concept, rather than simply seeing it as another flavor of strategy development.

The second section is intended to provide some tools and frameworks that can help business and design begin to apply the experience design concept at strategic and tactical levels. These tools and frameworks are ones that we have either adapted or developed over the years with a focus on establishing shared views on framing problems and evaluating solutions. We think that both the business-minded and the design-minded will find value in these as they help frame problems in ways that allow you to take an experience design approach to solving them. Chapter 5, which leads off this section, addresses how brand can be integrated into design in ways that go deeper than simply applying a logo or following brand guidelines. The goal is to unlock brand from mere branding and give a rationale for how to plan for reinforcing brand meaning, as well as how brand can help drive innovation. Chapter 6 provides ways of ensuring that products and services deliver upon and reinforce the meaning of the brand and discusses how taking an experience design approach can help identify options that should be planned for, even if they aren't used immediately. Chapter 7 presents a way to look at the entire customer life cycle with the goals of both creating a more holistic and seamless experience and planning how to more effectively engage customers. The section closes with Chapter 8, which suggests how the thinking behind the tools and frameworks in this section can be integrated within an overall experience design perspective.

The third and final section is focused on enabling business to begin to adapt and put experience design thinking into action internally and in their collaboration with design. In Chapter 9, we suggest ways of beginning to educate businesses on how to use experience design thinking in a broader sense than just for design projects. We talk about how to begin to grow internal advocates and get experience design working before design even occurs. Chapter 10 focuses on how experience design can change how and when to engage an external partner and what kind of engagement models work best and why.

Final Thoughts before Starting

We didn't set out to write this book with the hope of it being the next big thing, nor do we believe that business needs to understand what we are saying and implement immediately (or not—at its own peril). This isn't a justification for why our company is the logical design partner for your next design project or an annotated historical overview of the work we've done for our clients.

We were drawn to the design profession because we loved how form and function could be balanced and how doing this successfully also reflected the application of natural curiosity, empathy, and appreciation for the power of systems. It's a very humanist profession—in our eyes, the perfect balance of the rational and the creative. Perhaps best of all, there is never a shortage of problems against which one can apply oneself.

This book is not meant to be an argument for business to hand the keys of the kingdom over to design. In fact, we think that would probably be the exact wrong thing to do, because design is just beginning to become aware of the changes in thinking and approach that it needs to take. But we've also become aware that for design to make this change, we need to help our customers understand why this change also makes sense for them, and need both sides—design and business—to start a new conversation that reflects the times we live in and the future we currently see ahead.

Section I
Context

The execution of an action by no means proves that we know, even superficially, what we are doing or how we are doing it.

If we attempt to carry out an action with awareness—that is, to follow it in detail— we soon discover that even the simplest and most common of actions, such as getting up from a chair, is a mystery, and that we have no idea at all how it is done.

—Moshé Feldenkrais[1]

Moshé Feldenkrais was a Ukrainian-born, French-educated physicist who helped the British improve sonar during World War II and later developed an approach to physical therapy that he practiced after moving to Tel Aviv in 1954. Feldenkrais therapy is a form of physical therapy that begins with raising self-awareness in how movement is occurring and then using this awareness and a gentle guiding of new ways of moving to overcome physical problems. Modern understanding of the relationship between the brain and the body acknowledges that the body is capable of much movement, completely independent of conscious thought or even any awareness of what is actually going on. To some degree, there may even be aspects of movement that are hardwired outside of the "thinking" brain.

Before any change can begin, there needs to be an awareness of a current state from which one is changing. A lot of what we see as customer experience, and how business approaches it, seems to be based on a response that is largely going through the motions. It's something that everyone does, and often you simply improve what you did before or look around and see what others are doing and adopt aspects of it. The nature of the relationship between business and design that this creates also seems to occur without a real awareness of what's actually going on. Much of our thinking about experience design is based on the belief in the appropriateness (and necessity) of asking, "Why?" Why do we do things the way that we do?

There's a story we heard about a behavioral study in which five monkeys were put in a room with a banana hanging from the ceiling by a string. The only other thing in the room was a chair, which was high enough that a monkey standing on the chair could reach the banana. There was also a way for the observing team to spray the monkeys with ice-cold water if they tried to stand on the chair to reach the banana.

A short time after the monkeys had been trying to get the banana and after all had been uncomfortably soaked, the monkeys started to get wise. They stopped climbing on the chair. The researchers would then remove one of the monkeys and bring a new one in. Whenever the new member would try to go for the banana, the others would prevent it from getting on the chair. After a period of rotations, all of the monkeys who were in the first round had been replaced, yet the remaining monkeys would prevent any newly introduced monkey from climbing on the chair, even though none had firsthand experience of being sprayed with the cold water.

This story is based on a real research experiment, although the way the experiment was conducted was slightly different and the results weren't quite as dramatic as the version of the story we heard led us to believe. But when we first heard the story, it was easy to laugh with a sense of recognition and acknowledgment—we have all seen analogies of this kind of behavior in people (including ourselves). We sometimes ask clients why they believe a particular line of thinking is appropriate to follow and how they know that the situation they're in is the same as the one in which the original thinking was applied. Often, they can't really answer (in most cases they recognize the fallacy of assuming that it does).

The purpose of this section is to provide some context around the influences that informed our approach to experience design, followed by the basic components of experience design itself. This background will help bring meaning to the frameworks and tools in Section II, which will help ground your efforts as you begin to experiment with integrating brand, experience, value, and changing the way that business and design collaborate within a given situation. By providing a solid understanding of how we arrived at our approach, we aim to make these frameworks and tools both accessible and effective to use.

UNIVERSITY OF WINCHESTER
LIBRARY

1

Thinking about Design

Dogs flew spaceships!
The Aztecs invented the vacation!
Men and women are the same sex!
Our forefathers took drugs!
Your brain is not the boss!
Yes! That's right!
Everything you know is wrong!

—The Firesign Theatre, *Everything You Know Is Wrong* (1974)[1]

Samuel Arbesman believes that over the course of a lifetime, much of what one knows will lose relevance. It will either be shown to be incorrect, or it simply won't have any purpose, as the overall context will change so much that many "facts" will essentially become useless. In the fascinating book *The Half-Life of Facts: Why Everything We Know Has an Expiration Date*, he describes a kind of myopia that affects our understanding of knowledge and the world we live in. He calls this condition *shifting baseline syndrome* and describes it as follows[2]:

> This condition . . . shifting baseline syndrome . . . refers to how we become used to whatever state of affairs is true when we are born, or when we first look at a situation.

His point is that it's easy to take the ways things are for granted. We assume they have always been this way and will likely remain that way in the future. This can fool us into believing that there is some objective logic or rationale for why things are the way they are and that we can reliably build on that interpretation. A healthy counterview to shifting baseline syndrome is that the world is in constant flux and probably a lot less linear and serial than we think. What exists today is circumstantial, driven by influences we may not see, and therefore should not be assumed as being the right, or only, way to look at things.

What does shifting baseline syndrome have to do with design? One of the hallmarks of the designer mind-set is a natural curiosity about why things are the way they are. Which assumptions should be explored because they might be more limiting than beneficial? What emerging information and practices can be acquired and used to expand our understanding of how the designs of tomorrow will be different from those of today? This should be relevant to business as well because design helps create the value that businesses bring to their customers.

For our purposes, the important point is that things have not always been as they are today, and the current relationship between business and design is stuck in the past. It doesn't necessarily represent the best approach moving forward.

Kjetil Fallan is a faculty member at University of Oslo, in the Department of Philosophy, Classics, History of Art and Ideas. In *Design History: Understanding Theory and Method*, he makes the point that the current state of design may not be an optimized one[3]:

> Although the world never was as simple and neatly defined as it might appear in retrospect, there can be little doubt that the massive changes in industrial structures, manufacturing technologies, market organization, consumer behaviors, communication technologies, visualization techniques and so on over the past few decades are of vast importance for the restructuring of design practice.

We agree. Certainly the rate of change of nearly everything over the past few decades has accelerated greatly. The kinds of work and the nature of the problems that designers work on have shifted as a result. We find it useful to look further back than the past few decades to understand what has led up to the situation today and why this recent increase in the frequency of change is so important for what business and design do together in the future.

Over the past few centuries there's been a transition in the objectives of design and who provides it. In fact, an entire field is devoted to design history. We're not going to review the theories and approaches here. It's a worthwhile subject we recommend perusing sometime, and it's certainly relevant to the practice of design analysis. But we couldn't do it justice and still focus on more relevant issues, such as the future of how business and design work together, in a single volume. That said, a little perspective is useful, especially for those who are less familiar with design.

But before we look back, we should make sure that we all have the same view of what we mean when we say *design*. To have a meaningful discussion of how business and design should be looking at each other's worlds and working together, we need a common understanding of design and the role it plays to realize that what we take for granted about design has not always been the case.

As we consider design and what is changing in the role that design plays in business and everyday life, we will also point out the emerging importance of time. With the increased rate of change in technology today, products have increasingly shorter life spans. Services deliver time-based value, and that value must be evident to people to make them feel like they should continue to pay for it. Likewise, businesses look to translate their brand values into lasting relationships with customers that not only allow a business to exist, but with luck, allow it to grow. In fact, we see the role that time plays in design as being a large component of experience design. The benefit is that a deeper consideration of time across multiple interconnected areas of a business and customer relationship allows for better leverage of systemic qualities that design can provide and the ability to plan for options without the cost of fully committing to them—all with one common objective: keeping the customer engaged by providing value.

The Duality of Design

Look at this book—the texture and size of the pages, the words on the page, the diagrams, and the cover art (or the e-book reader you are holding and the way that it allows you to flip "pages" and change the size of the type to better suit your eyesight). Every aspect of what you see was designed. Now look around the room you're in (or the vehicle, if you are travelling). Consider how many discrete objects there are and how many people and how much time was involved in creating them. We live in a designed world, yet we rarely think about it.

Some believe that design is responsible merely for why things look the way they do. Every human-made object we encounter in our lives has an appearance, and at some point in the process of creating it, someone made a decision—intentionally or not—that would affect how it would look. Most of us are familiar with (and may actually use) the phrase *form follows function*. Even many things that we think of as being in their "natural" state have been visually altered to look the way they do, and in many cases, this is highly intentional (for instance, when we see meat, sugar, rice, leather, landscapes, and people, we take it for granted that they are always in their natural state, but they aren't; perhaps we should be slightly uncomfortable in the way the form/function model gets applied these days). It's pretty easy for us to form an intuitive sense about what design is, based on the fact that we can see it all around us. Even so, we can forget that *everything* is designed, not just designer furniture and fashion clothing. With so many examples like these, it's easy to think that design as it relates to appearance is what determines the cost of things, especially because the most expensive things seem to have very conspicuous designs. We are delighted when we find a more ordinary object—a tea kettle, an iron, a broom—that strikes us as "designed" but is very affordable, perhaps not much more expensive than other "nondesigned" variations of the same product. Many businesses have become successful by realizing this and providing affordable design.

This role of arbiter of appearances is an important one for design to play for a very simple reason: We are visual animals. Sight is the predominant way that we relate to the world around us. We may be attracted by a wonderful smell, but we would rarely eat anything without first looking at it. When we hear something, we look to see where the noise is coming from to understand the significance of the noise—should we investigate, ignore, or run like hell?

Although we develop the sense of hearing very early in development, we see well before we can use or understand language. We may first learn of many things through words, written and spoken, but it's all the more real when we see whatever it is for the first time. For humans, seeing is believing. And our natural cognitive reaction to seeing something is to focus on the object to derive meaning from what we see.

So attributing the reasons that things look the way that they do to design is useful. Certainly one role of design is to make objects have more value within their context of use (this includes functional, financial, cultural, and social contexts). But it's not the full picture. It suggests that design is a final step; a wrapper, or a container, or the presentation. In this position, design occurs toward the end stages of the process of planning and making objects. This is only half the story. *Design* is not just a noun; *design* is also a verb—a process. It is the thinking and the actions that go into producing the final design. A good way to understand the importance of this noun/verb connection is through procedural description, so here's a scenario:

Imagine you are housesitting for a friend who has a small woodshop in his basement. He knows you're the creative sort and has encouraged you to build something. He has left three blocks of wood on the worktable for you. Each block of wood is a 12-inch cube; one is white pine, one is bird's-eye maple, and one is cedar. Under the worktable, you also find a fully stocked toolbox, a tape measure, and some glue. There's a complicated-looking table saw in the corner, along with some other machinery that you aren't quite sure about. After turning the saw on for a second, the noise quickly convinces you that having all of your fingers properly attached to your hand is probably a better idea than fooling around with dangerous machinery.

Your mind begins to wander through things that are made of wood and stops with . . . a box. A box should be pretty easy. You think that maybe a jewelry box would be nice. You'll give it to your significant other and maybe even buy something nice and sparkling to put inside for extra points. You choose the maple block, which has a beautiful grain. Deciding that you'll cut it into sections from which you'll construct the box, you get to work. Your phone buzzes with a text from your significant other, but you justify not responding for now: You are in the middle of a labor of love. After a lot of labor and not much progress or love, you realize that the maple is extremely hard. You persevere. But as you continue, you realize it's really difficult to keep the cuts even, and you aren't too happy with the results. You begin to rethink things and are pretty convinced the effort with this block is going to produce something a whole lot less impressive than you imagined. Even so, one hour and a ruined block of wood later, you are undaunted with your original mission of building a box.

Starting again, you grab the cedar block and try cutting it. The saw goes through quickly, and your cuts are much better. Before you know it, you have a bunch of 12 × 12 × ¾-inch boards. The wood is not as pretty as the maple, though. You wonder if a jewelry box is the best thing to make. Maybe a cigar box (for yourself) would be a better choice than a jewelry box (for your other half). Besides, this way you won't have to also buy a piece of jewelry. You realize that you need to cut some of the pieces down into smaller sizes so the box doesn't look like a 12-inch cube. After (somewhat randomly) deciding that it will be 12 inches long by 4 inches high by 6 inches deep, you set out to cut the pieces up into sides, a top, and a bottom. Now you begin to put the pieces together to form the basic box.

Do the sides bookend the front and back or vice versa? After brief consideration, you decide that the sides will bookend the front and back. But how will you attach them? Looking around you see some small wooden crates on the floor. Inspecting them, you notice that the sides are held together with what look like small nails. You see some small nails in the toolbox and decide that these will do. As you maneuver the boards in a way that allows you to drive the nail to join the first side to the front, you swing the hammer and gently tap the nail. The wood splits.

No worries; you have extra pieces that you can cut to replace the split one. Rather than make the same mistake again, though, you decide to use the drill and screws, thinking this will prevent splitting. After a while, you realize that you can't drill a hole through the side and into the edge of the front at the same time, so you do it one at a time. As you're screwing the pieces together, you realize the holes are in slightly different places in relation to the board edges. Although you've joined the two pieces together, the edges are not flush. You still have more wood, so you take some measurements and cut some more pieces. This time, the two boards are joined and flush (or at least close enough)!

Your phone buzzes again. Another text from you-know-who, but you're on a mission and ignore this one, too. You continue until you have all four sides of the box joined together. Excited, you now get ready to put the bottom on. This should be easy because you can lay it on top of the sides and then drill through the edges of the sides to ensure a good fit. Unfortunately, you cut the bottom and top to be 12 × 6 inches and now realize that the box is actually 13.5 inches long (the sides each added ¾ inch to the length). None of the wood is long enough (12 inches maximum length), so you decide that the bottom will be "inside" the sides.

As you try to move forward with this plan, you realize that the inner dimensions are not 12 × 6 inches but 12 × 4½ inches (the front and back each now take up ¾ inch of the original 6-inch width). You cut 1½ inches off the bottom, apply the glue to its edges, and then place the box so that the bottom is now inside. Now you see that the last saw cut wasn't exactly straight, leaving a bit of a gap. No problem. Glue will fill that, and as you squeeze glue liberally into the gap, you remember a line you once heard—glue, putty, sandpaper, and paint make a carpenter all that he ain't! Once it dries, you plan to drill through the sides and into the bottom and set the screws. Happy with your progress, you decide to go upstairs and relax while the glue sets.

After rewarding yourself with a refreshing drink for doing such a good job, you return to find that the glue has set. You also find that the box is now stuck to the worktable. You start prying and pushing the box to free it, and then—*snap!*—one of the sides breaks along the grain, which you now realize is probably running the wrong way. You hadn't really thought about the grain and strength of the wood when you cut the block. At this point, cursing, you throw it all away. A second block of wood is wasted, and the better part of the day is gone. But armed with your new experience, and perhaps a little obsessed, you start anew and grab the white pine block.

Your phone rings, and you see it's your significant other again, calling this time instead of texting and ticked that you didn't reply earlier. You let it go to voice mail because now you've hit your stride.

By now, you know a lot more about what to do and, more important, what not to do, so it goes much faster and you're ready to put the top on only a few hours later. Of course, finishing this is a little tricky. You hadn't thought about the fact that the hinges need to be recessed or the lid won't lay flat. You go with the only other option and put them outside on the back of the box. Not as nice looking—they stick over the top a little—but it's done! Your new humidor is finished. You make a little humidifier by placing a damp sponge in a plastic container you found in the kitchen, with a few holes poked in its lid and sides, and adding that to your humidor.

Back at home a few days later, you notice black stains have formed in the wood of your handmade box. Mildew! You realize that the mildew-resistant cedar may have been the best choice after all and are annoyed that the cedar box broke. Giving up your fantasy of quitting your day job and opening a little wood shop to make and sell your handmade boxes, you decide to treat yourself and purchase a well-made humidor.

Now you have learned something about production and design. If you were more experienced at using the tools and going through the process, it would have been easier. You have the appreciation for the craft. And, if you had known what you wanted to make before you started, you could have planned the entire process in advance, including the box dimensions, type of wood, joinery techniques—every aspect could have been thought through. You could have computed all the measurements and set the order of assembly, all based on the end goal, the materials available, and your craft skills. You could have even considered different approaches to the size and construction, weighing the trade-offs between them and the relative merits of each finished product before you started.

You realize that you could have and should have designed the box before you produced the final outcome in order to increase the odds of having something useful and desirable. With the knowledge you now have, you know exactly how each aspect of the design (appearance) would have related both to the process of making the box as well as its value to someone once made.

Although this example may seem overly contrived, it does illustrate the duality and interdependence of each side of the concept of design. It also illustrates that underestimating the importance of design as a process can lead to problems. Appreciating this duality is critical to understanding how business can get the most out of design and why the current relationship between the two often doesn't produce the level of value that it could. When business provides an incomplete description of what is needed or design is not familiar enough with the process and the implication on what kinds of questions should be asked, the results may be rather disappointing. It's easy to underestimate how long the right solution will take when important information only becomes available after some level of effort has already been made.

This scenario is also illuminating in another way. It illustrates a subtle but very important nuance. The intention of the effort—the choice of what to make, for whom, and why—shifted during the course of the scenario, but only as a result of mistakes being made. This occurred largely because of the lack of a good design, which would have ensured that the process produced the right outcome. The final product and its overall effect on you and your partner were larger than just a box of dubious quality. The outcome was arguably even less successful than no box at all. The process of making the box and the usefulness of the finished product existed inside other processes and relationships that weren't fully considered.

Matthew B. Crawford writes about the value of craft and how modern production processes remove the connection to making value that people once had. He sees the process of work as important to the quality of the output because of the information one gains and the resulting knowledge that arises during the process. In his book, *Shop Class as Soulcraft*, he writes[4]:

> Knowing what kind of problem you have on hand means knowing what features of the situation can be ignored. Even the boundaries of what counts as "the situation" can be ambiguous; making discriminations of pertinence cannot be achieved by the application of rules, and requires the kind of judgment that comes with experience.

When we start thinking about the role of design in producing value for paying customers, the duality in the concept—process and outcome—starts to apply itself to a range of different areas, many of which are beyond the scope of the specific designed object. The problem is that it's really difficult to think through all of the different vectors and relationships that can help us understand the importance of each and the interdependencies between them. This is often because we aren't aware of them until after it's too late, and their absence is what brings them brings them to our attention.

The essence of this challenge is touched upon by the design historian Hazel Conway as she shows how easy it is to lay out the different avenues that connect design and object[5]:

> Another confusion lies in the interpretation of the word "design." When we talk about the design of a lamp, for example, we may be concerned with the mental processes and the drawings and models that eventually result in that particular lamp; we may be concerned with the production process, the form and material of the lamp and how it is used; we could also be concerned with how the lamp was marketed, advertised, packaged and sold.

If you believe that design is important because it affects customers' overall perception of value—which it does—then design is a much more complex concept to fully manage. That's because now every objective requires the right process, outcome, and understanding of the larger context in which it will exist. This is a key point and is foundational to the experience design approach we put forth in this book. Unlike pure innovation, which may be targeted at identifying emerging or unrealized needs, and unlike design thinking, which grounds the design criteria in the real world of the user needs and behaviors, experience design incorporates all disciplines of and approaches to design into an awareness of how to build systems that support customers in receiving value by recognizing that it's never just about the single object or the current project requirements and parameters.

Modern businesses have many moving parts required for delivering value to customers, and experience design can become a way to see how these efforts relate to one another. It provides a framework for looking at how they reinforce core brand values and how decisions, which need to be made in the process of design, can have a further reaching effect than simply what the product looks and feels like.

But why is it so easy to ignore even the basic duality of design? Why is there a tendency to believe that letting business priorities dictate design objectives produces a better outcome than asking someone with a maker/designer mind-set to solve the problem in a viable way? We believe that the evolution of the relationship between business and design has a lot to do with it.

Design: The Evolutionary Advantage

The propensity to design is in our human nature and has probably been there for a long, long time. Many theories on human intelligence, the evolution of the brain as the source of and reason for our unique form of consciousness, take the point of view that there is an advantage to being able to model different scenarios in our heads before committing ourselves to actions. In essence, we are probably hardwired for design. But it gets even more interesting.

When you think about design and what's involved in designing, it's natural to think about the role that the hand plays. If it's the craftsman's eye that determines what excellence is in a product, surely it's the craftsman's hands that make it happen. Frank Wilson is a neurologist who treats people who have sustained work-related hand injuries. He has been fascinated with the hand-brain relationship in human evolution and the role this relationship has played in defining the world we live in today. In his book, *The Hand*, he lays out this story, in which he ties the development of the hand and the systems required to control it to our success as bipeds, the ability for toolmaking and technology, and the development of language—essentially making the point that our humanness is as much related to our hands as to our brains.

Wilson clearly believes that the hand-brain connection is an important aspect of our humanity, writing[6]:

> I would argue that any theory of human intelligence which ignores the interdependence of hand and brain function, the historic origins of that relationship, or the impact of that history on developmental dynamics in modern humans, is grossly misleading and sterile.

The importance of the hand to design is clear. Earlier, we said that sight is extremely important and perhaps the primary way that we receive our world. Another primary way that we exercise our minds in an attempt to interact with our world is through the use of our hands. It's true that we interact based on our presence, our voice, our hands, and the rest of our bodies, but the multipurpose tool that gives us the most bang for the buck is the hand.

Wilson is not alone in seeing the hand-brain connection. Lewis Wolpert, a professor of Biology Applied to Medicine at University College in London, believes that humans are unique in our ability to make tools based on observation, planning, and iterative refinement. Although other animals may use tools, most only do so by taking existing objects and using them with very little if any modification. And the tools are generally not reused, nor is tool use taught; rather, it is mimicked in most cases.[7]

He sees that there are a few interesting implications arising from this observation. One is that the "technology" of a tool can be shared, passed down across generations, and improved. The other is his hypothesis that the ability to identify and model cause, effect, and implication, which is needed for tool building (and design for everything from a scenario for stealing bananas to developing computers), is also the same mechanism on which belief systems are built. Belief systems will resurface later in the book as we discuss business, design, and the emergence of modern branding.

The Maker/Designer

It seems fairly plausible that humans have evolved the way we have largely based on internal mechanisms that allow us to think, share, build, and control our world via this bidirectional world-hand-brain connection. As a species, we shape the things that shape our existence.

And throughout much of this time, grappling with the duality of design while balancing the process and end goal was the responsibility of the maker. Much of what was produced by people for themselves and others was based on an intuitive "design" that was influenced primarily by the materials, the most efficient ways of working with these materials, and the requirements of end use (utility and durability). Any additional aesthetic choices reflected broader social and cultural values and possibly the tastes and personality of the maker. The maker's identity became a useful symbol of value, but often these were not outwardly visible as being separate from attributes related to function and social/cultural values. A maker's mark might have existed on an unobtrusive spot somewhere on the product.

For things that required time and specialized knowledge to produce, there was an advantage to finding someone who could produce it faster and better than one could do for oneself. Sometimes producing specialized things involved a division of labor, such as different workstations for different stages of production of stone tools and weapons.

We have come a long way since groups of early humans sat together and shared the task of chipping stone into weapons—or maybe we haven't. Wilson discusses the universal way that this division of labor approach works in his book. He makes this point in a way that brings amusing stereotypes to mind[8]:

> Silicon Valley designers and engineers conceptualize, design, test, and perfect electronic machines in a process that is indistinguishable from that seen in Aborigines in stone and tool manufacture . . .

Enabling skilled craftsmen to benefit from knowledge guilds and similar craft-centric organizations functioned as a way of both leveraging the knowledge through the labor of others and protecting proprietary techniques. The labor-for-knowledge value exchange also helped transfer skills from person to person when media channels and educational institutions didn't exist to fill that role for the masses. (Another probable benefit of this structure was that the most knowledgeable and experienced workers could also push the technology forward, through experimentation, while the less skilled workers produced the bulk of the work that paid the bills.) A scalable maker/designer approach was a predominant way to produce things of value for others.

We admit that this is a very coarse-grained overview that doesn't consider centuries of social, cultural, political, and economic change, but there are some pragmatic reasons why a smart design-minded species would evolve into this kind of structure for managing design expertise in the creation of value.

First, to have production and design sensibilities reside in the minds of different individuals requires the ability of those individuals to communicate aspects of design. For much of human history, communication technologies have been somewhat limited—not everyone could read or write. If design is to be something that can be shared beyond the process of making, it has to be communicated in some way. You had to know how to read or write. You had to have time and access to materials used to record the knowledge, and others needed time to assimilate the knowledge and then practice it to a degree that allowed it to be perfected, thereby reaching the level of consistency necessary to ensure the application of the design produced value.

In *Antifragile*, Nassim Nicholas Taleb describes how a lot of the "engineering" details used by the ancients weren't necessarily formally documented. He explains that because so much resided in undocumented decision making, Roman bridge designers and their families were forced to live under the bridges they constructed; after all, no one would want to live under a bridge unless they were fairly certain it wasn't going to collapse on top of them.[9]

With the invention and evolution of the printing press, the ability to record and distribute information became more efficient. But it would be a while before printed information would have a large impact on the role that design played and how this would affect the maker/designer.

Second, the processes for making things were still largely manual. This meant the quality was dependent on the individual craftsman. There was no way to formalize the craftsman's knowledge and skill and embody it in a set of rules and behaviors that would allow it to be produced at large scale with the same level of quality across craftsmen or even from one piece to the next. This would not come into play in meaningful ways until the Industrial Revolution.

Third, and perhaps most important, the size and nature of markets was different. A good portion of the population did not have the means to acquire things beyond what was needed for mere subsistence. Transportation was not highly efficient, so producing more than could be sold locally was not economical if people in other markets made the same thing. There was neither demand nor a financial advantage for having design exist separate from the maker. Without some form of consumerism and the ability to mass-produce, the maker/designer was the optimal configuration. There was not enough need to differentiate, nor was the speed of consumption high enough to justify trying.

Splitting the Maker/Designer

During the Industrial Revolution, a series of technological advances streamlined the processes of manufacturing and production. Although these shifts happened over the course of a century and over two distinct waves of change, there were impacts to the maker/designer model of effectiveness.

In discussing the differences between craft and mass production, Matthew B. Crawford writes[10]:

> The craftsman is proud of what he has made, and cherishes it, while the consumer discards things that are perfectly serviceable in his restless pursuit of the new.

The first change that came about was that more products could be produced with the benefits of economy of scale, arising from more efficient means of generating power, better control over the replication of quality, and more throughput capacity in manufacturing. Manual labor was replaced with machines. It became easier to produce products, and once the knowledge of the maker/designer was instantiated in mechanical processes, the means of production became the main source of value for business (as opposed to the knowledge needed to produce a specific product).

Another shift was that the craft skills that were needed for production of one kind of product were often also fungible to other products. The skills needed for making a wheel for a wagon or other conveyance were similar to those needed for making a bicycle wheel. And Crawford points out that as the automobile began to replace these other forms of transportation, craftsmen who had the best all-around mechanical skills moved from producing one kind of product to producing another. In addition, the design and creation of the new production processes became a focus of many of the skill types who were once focused on designing/making end products themselves.

Two vectors of evolutionary change were now set in motion. The first: Access to capital would allow someone to buy the knowledge and means for production, without requiring very much in the way of experience from a maker/designer background. This meant that competition was now going to be driven by access to capital and to markets, not just knowledge of craft and level of quality. Second, it put any decision about what role design played, and why, into the hands of people who were weighing other considerations, such as profits and growth, as well—and often, these other factors were considered to be of equal or higher priority than design.

There were many areas in which the maker/designer mentality was still considered a high priority and key to how products were made and why people would want them. But even in these areas, there was a split between what was needed to make a product—and make it easy to manufacture—versus what was needed to make a product more valuable or desirable to a consumer. As Kjetil Fallan describes it, this split in maker/designer thinking can be categorized based on who benefits the most from the thinking[11]:

> When engineers design cog wheels to go in the power transmission of a drill or disc brakes for a car, it would seem material more at home in the history of technology than in design history. However, when engineers design drills or car bodies their work is of more immediate interest to design history. It may seem that the crux of the matter is the degree to which the object as an entity interacts directly with the users.

Back to our earlier discussion about how we interact with the world—presence, eyes, voice, hands. If the customer can't see it, doesn't need to touch it, and doesn't ask about it, why spend time on design? When it's the guts that most people don't see, don't understand, and rarely worry about, it's considered technology and sits within the primary objectives of business control. When it's things that people see, interact with, and make decisions about, it's design. And when production and design are separated, business can be tempted to buy design whenever and wherever it makes the most sense. Often, this dichotomy seems clear, and business confidently decides to go without external input from design. In our experience, it's almost never as simple as it may first appear. And often, the customer's experience is tied to a deeper connection than the surface appearance.

Information Accelerates Change

Another interesting and underappreciated shift that began to happen during the 1800s was the role that information began to play and how this ushered in the advent of consumerism. (It also set the stage for how crucial the increasingly rapid rate of information would be to business and what business would begin to look to design to provide.)

For instance, in discussing the changes in women's fashion during the Victorian era, Hazel Conway notes that what a woman wore was a strong indication of her class and status. As such, working-class women who aspired to hold a higher station would try to dress in a way that suggested they were more than they really were. The upward compression on those at the top meant that they needed to be wearing something new and different to reaffirm their position. As a result, people began to look at fashion trends circulating in print, in order to understand what they should be looking for.

Conway writes, "The proliferation of fashion journals at this time, with the minutest nuance of change being recorded, meant that ideas could rapidly be disseminated."[12]

While information's role in setting tastes and defining what sells certainly didn't start here, clearly the relationship between information and demand gets a healthy boost, as both the means to produce and distribute information in faster and more economical ways became available. In *A Publisher's History of American Magazines,* Peter Hutchinson points out that between 1800 and 1900, the literate population in the United States increased by a factor of 20. In 1800, only 13 magazines were published in the United States, compared with 3,500 in 1900, and more than 8.2 billion copies of magazines and newspapers were printed in 1900 (which, based on the 1900 census, equates to more than 100 for every citizen).[13]

As it becomes easier to produce products for markets with economies of scale and as it becomes easier to inform and affect consumers' understanding of what's available and what choice makes the most sense, those who control the capital to fund both sides of the supply/demand curve are now in a position to determine what gets made, for whom, and why. From this position, it's easy to assume control of how design is being used to identify, create, and deliver value—to the point where design can now be guided in terms of what is needed where and what criteria will be used to evaluate the outcome.

Codifying Design as Separate from Making

During the latter half of the nineteenth century, more and more products could be made in more economical ways. Much of the core value for a product could be produced with the necessary production knowledge instantiated in an optimized manufacturing process. Design implementation no longer required a maker/designer, at least not for products that could effectively be mass-produced. But not everyone was happy with the kind of aesthetic choices available through these manufactured products.

The concept of the balance between form and function is often attributed to William Morris, who owned a design business that, ironically, provided decorative ornamentation for church interiors. Morris was a founder of the Arts and Crafts movement that started in the 1860s and influenced art and ornamentation through the 1910s. Although the Arts and Crafts movement was largely a reaction to industrialization and its effects on the aesthetic and decorative choices being made in factories, its focus was on restoring a more natural influence to the hands of the craftsman, who was able to meld the nature of the material with art that reflected the mainstream cultural values (including the elevation of the natural world). The movement had an international influence on design, although it was not fully concerned with form and function in regard to economic value or the functional value of products.

At the same time that form and function became a topic that an end user might consider when purchasing a product, others involved in production and design were interested in how the rules and characteristics of form could be systematized toward true production and use value, thus moving away from the province of fine arts.

The Bauhaus movement in Germany (beginning after World War I and running until the beginning of World War II) took some of the philosophical underpinnings of the Arts and Crafts movement and began to express them in slightly more utilitarian ways. The founders of the movement were interested in bridging many disciplines involved in production and design as well as fine art. One of the goals was tying the process of design and manufacturing to ownership and use. By using design as a way to optimize form and function as well as production, the common man would be able to more broadly enjoy the fruits of design. The choice of form was no longer tied only to decoration and ornamentation but also directly to what made a product better to use and easier to produce.

This movement produced some very influential thinkers and practitioners. It also helped formalize design systems—that is, which formal elements and attributes were important and why and the different ways in which the elements of design could be systematically considered and managed. Modern book design, modern typefaces, modern product design, and modern architecture—many aspects that we take for granted today as being what design is about—came into use during this time. In fact, the Bauhaus style was often referred to as international style, because the aesthetic choices were not tied to specific cultures or historical influences of fine arts. Graphic design, which is primarily concerned with information, meaning, and effective communication in two-dimensional media (think print), was greatly influenced by this movement.

The formalization of design systems as knowledge that could be applied, separated from, and considered even before the actual production of a product began allowed the design professions to be freed from having to make things in order to influence them. Designers could consult or design in abstract, becoming more like the modern designer of today: often having a set of highly perfected skills and looking for a problem to apply them against. It also meant that business could begin to evaluate what aspects of design they believed were most appropriate, because the design and production were now only as integrated as the business and product required them to be. Suddenly, design was much less connected to production.

The Modern Brand

We mentioned that information was accelerating the rate of change in many ways, especially in regard to how people learned about products and prevailing tastes. Information about design processes and techniques could be captured and communicated. Those who were buying and using products could now see options before deciding to buy. Although advertising had been around for quite a while, there was a host of new, financially viable vehicles to promote new products, including published magazines, newspapers, catalogs, and so on. An emerging connection between business, production, demand, and the rise of consumerism set the stage for an interesting shift in how information drove markets and how business used design.

Brands have been around for a long time. People often used symbols that stood for their products or their lineage, which may have had a relationship to the creation and purveyance of certain products. But modern branding really came into its own in the twentieth century. The ability to economically put a message in front of a consumer; the emergence of products that you could buy, rather than make yourself; and the pursuit of profits based on the economies of scale provided by manufacturing and communication began to suggest that creating a reason why someone should buy your product (as opposed to a competitor's) were good things.

As Crawford describes it[14]:

> Consumption, no less than production, needed to be brought under scientific management—the management of desire. Thus, there came to be marketers who called themselves "consumption engineers" in the early decades of the twentieth century.

In describing the rise of modern advertising and branding and the role they play in giving context and meaning to society, James Twitchell makes a connection between the dynamics of religious belief systems and the mechanisms behind brand building. In his book, *Adcult USA*, he talks about early pioneers of advertising in the twentieth century as having been very familiar with the practice of religion. Some had even been clergy or divinity students.[15]

What seemed to click for these early pioneers of positioning and messaging was an understanding of belief systems and how, once established, such a belief system became a very powerful force for affecting people's behavior. The more universal a value provided by a belief system's foundation, the more powerful it could be in motivating a person to do specific kinds of things. And people seemed to respond to being asked to operate on blind faith if the belief was strong enough.

If you remember our discussion of value in the Introduction, we talked about three types: tangible, intangible, and aspirational. The tangible value of almost anything can easily be demonstrated by comparing what it's supposed to do with how capable it is of performing that feat. But intangible and aspirational value are often abstract, represented through ideals to be taken on faith until you're able to realize them for yourself (and implicitly, in your own subjective way).

These ideals represented by brands were tied into social and cultural needs and aspirations. People were interested in profiting from the advantages of technology, living the good life, and being happy and prosperous. Brands could represent their ideals and values into design attributes that could be layered onto products. By "layered" we mean that changes to the appearance and secondary features could be made without significantly affecting the process or cost of production (it could just as easily stop at the packaging and advertisements). Although design wasn't literally translating these into specific components of utility in the product, it could help make the brand differentiation visually "real" and apparent, and advertising was the perfect vehicle for carrying the message.

This was the new area of value that became important for driving consumerism and taking advantage of the ease of production unleashed during the Industrial Revolution. And there was a nice tie-in to other areas of culture that were commonly used in conveying these kinds of intangible and aspirational ideas: the graphic and fine arts. With channels of communication available to businesses and a public that was beginning to look at the media in these channels for cues on how to think, act, and buy, the modern brand began to take shape. Here, design played a role in developing something for business that was not tied to the process of making products, because what was being designed were ideas, concepts, values, and principles in the abstract. Although they referred to the product, the design of the presentation of this information had little to do with the design of the product.

The choices of how to portray these kinds of ideals had little pragmatic constraint. The designer could work with a system of design components that were highly flexible but capable of being combined in specific ways to create very unique and eventually proprietary design systems or brand identities. The values of the brand were to be represented by the choice of elements and their systemic application by a designer, who needed no real or practical knowledge of the product or how it worked or was produced. The people buying design didn't need to have that knowledge either. Yet this relationship between business and design could be very powerful. For instance, although Coca-Cola was established as a brand before this transition began to happen in full, Coke did leverage this shift. We still experience the power of this every year. The modern version of Santa Claus, the color of red used then (and still today), and to a certain extent, the consumerism inherent in the modern version of this holiday were all inspired by ads commissioned by the company for its brand. As Hazel Conway describes it, we are aware that this is happening, yet we are unaware how deeply this may affect us[16]:

> In the streets, in the shops, reading the papers or magazines, or watching television, advertisements designers hope to have a direct effect on us, and this we recognize. Their indirect effects are, however, much more subtle and not nearly so easy to recognize, yet our perception of ourselves, our surroundings and our society are affected by them.

This represents a fundamental shift away from the maker/designer model in which the duality of design was mediated through individual decisions based on how the needs of the two sides (process/final artifact) should best be served. Now business was in the driver's seat and could use a more scientific approach to streamlining production and driving demand, with brand being the emerging point of focus for the consumer. In this situation, design's biggest effect would be felt in how the brand was brought to life and used; the decisions about product were no longer open and flexible, and consumers' attention was often diverted away from the pragmatic tangible value of the product in favor of the intangible and aspirational value of the brand.

Where There's Brand, There's Consumerism

With the end of World War II, a lot of new technology was making its way from the military industrial complex into consumer products. There was also a lot of manufacturing capacity and a lot of people who were entering the workforce, both to help the supply side and to be paid salaries to drive the demand side. Consumerism finally had all the right pieces to fully take off.

Add to this new and more effective channels of mass media, and you have the perfect situation for business. With new materials and design disciplines such as industrial design, you could now create basic models that used the same manufacturing process and components but evolved through a series of small design changes, each one an improvement on the previous. Design could leverage the business's brand values to create incremental change in appearances and features for products, which helped business create consumption cycles in which the consumer could gratify the entire range of value (tangible, intangible, and aspirational) on an ongoing basis. In many cases the only thing that really changed was how design was appealing to the intangible and the aspirational. The fact that the process of making things was optimized for cost of production, and not necessarily product durability, certainly helped (and consumers began to suspect that some products even had built-in obsolescence). Because the target of brand belief was deeper than rationality, the whole mechanism could become instilled in society to the point where the advertisements and branded products weren't serving preexisting needs as much as defining what was important and desirable. It's quite a feat for a business to not only have the means for producing supply but also have access to the means for producing demand. When you can connect the two, the nature of the market changes. Customers become consumers on a treadmill, with increasing opportunities to acquire more value of all kinds.

We feel compelled to highlight a couple of interesting points that arise out of this state of affairs—points that differ from what existed in previous centuries. For starters, technological change affected how business and design worked together, enabling a separation between design and production. Second, the role that design played in creating or enhancing value when business chose to use design. And third, the question of what to make, for whom, and why could now be decided without consulting design—until after the fact—by convincing people that they should buy something because of its subjective value.

This state of the relationship between business and design was relatively well optimized for its time, but it wasn't the only road to take, nor was it the best. We arrived there largely because no one really had to think about it along the way. As Samuel Arbesman would say, "We are not well equipped for slow change."[17]

Acceleration through Technology

The latter half of the twentieth and beginning of the current century saw a new wrinkle in the collaboration of business and design. The development of computing and network technologies, along with the general growth of the economy, created new areas within the service economy. In addition, services previously provided by people could now become productized as software. The Internet created a new channel for connecting media and services to consumers. Many services shifted to IP-based networks. All of this led to new areas of design, specifically, the emergence of interface and interaction design.

The three new kinds of business concerns in which design became involved were digital media (websites, content), digital services (applications, e-commerce, media services), and digital marketing (ads, e-mail, microsites). Suddenly, the business and the customer could actually interact directly in real time through the final designs of any digital product or service. This shift also altered the relationship of the process and outcome of design, because the role that time plays became much more important to consider. Figure 1.1 shows just some of the variables that need to be considered before design can even begin to create a service experience that would work for customers.

Unlike a physical product, a digital product (or service) had a lot of the content and controls presented visually through a screen. Because the screen contents were

Figure 1.1
Five Basic Areas Digital Design
Takes into Account

A

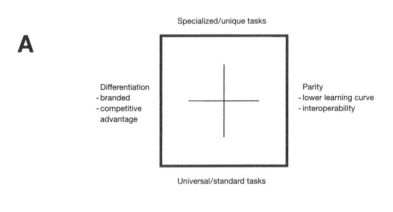

Specialized/unique tasks

Differentiation
- branded
- competitive
 advantage

Parity
- lower learning curve
- interoperability

Universal/standard tasks

B

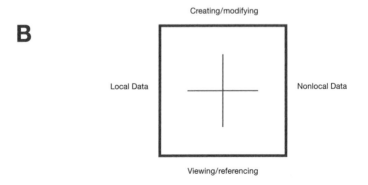

Creating/modifying

Local Data

Nonlocal Data

Viewing/referencing

C

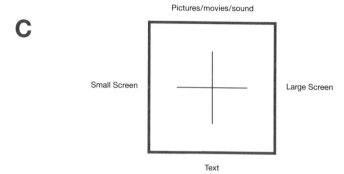

D

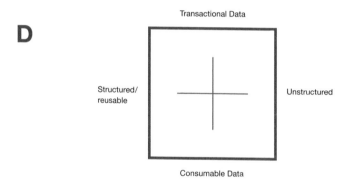

E

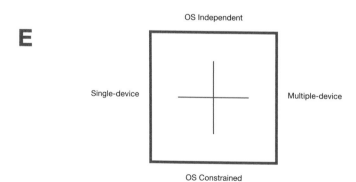

generated by the hardware inside, what was on the screen could change over time. In addition, many of these products had a lot of features and capabilities that were provided by the internal components (not how the product was physically used), which meant that users had to invest time in learning what was there and how to use it. When these products and services also provided a bidirectional flow of data from the product to someone else and back again, the nature of the value provided could change over time. Finally, because of the technical architecture of digital products and services, not only could products have their value proposition "updated" over time, but the options for different kinds of solutions could change as new technologies changed what was possible. When a current standard of efficiency for a product becomes outmoded, it's very difficult to build a case for staying with it.

When computing systems first began to utilize graphical user interfaces, one of the emerging concerns was that there needed to be some kind of mediation between the system and the user that acknowledged the human way of experiencing the world. User-centered design was the approach suggested, and a lot of design for the digital medium was evaluated for usability as a primary criteria. With the combination of this user-centricity and the relative novelty of the problem space (and scarcity of experienced practitioners), the business side began to allow—and in some cases rely on—design to provide the maker/designer benefits.

With several decades of experience under their belt, many businesses began to invest in taking some of the management and development of the digital channels and services in-house, at least at the data and core service level. New tools allowed for certain areas of design to be executed by anyone willing to learn how to use them. And the proliferation of options and examples for how these tools could be used allowed for novelties that were of more interest than strict adherence to the user-centric conventions of predictable usability. Businesses wanted design to create experiences that were much more dynamic and that differentiated their story by taking advantage of the medium in innovative ways. Often, a business would ask design to improve the user interface or create an innovative experience. In some cases, design staff for digital media were embedded in business's functional units, when benefits of a real maker/designer approach were needed. But despite all these variations in where design staff sat, it was still business that largely determined what, when, and why, often from very tactical perspectives. Design became a stage gate. In many cases, the relationship between a business and an external design partner was managed much the same way that an internal design staff was managed. In many cases, the choice to go outside was driven by capacity and access to particular levels of expertise, but it didn't necessarily change who made what decisions. In many ways this had to be because the outside partner was working with the internal teams to some degree.

There was also a new breed of business that needed design: the Internet start-up. These were marked by several characteristics. The first was the belief that change was inevitable and would sweep people up (as customers) without much need to convince them to "buy." This often meant that the value the business was providing was obscure, in some cases apparent only to the founders and their investors. A second characteristic that was largely present only during the first wave of these new entities was deep pockets. Start-ups had raised significant amounts of capital. (The "later waves" had almost the exact opposite situation: clear value proposition but little capital.) A third characteristic was that they needed an entire company (brand, product/service, marketing, customer relationships) built ASAP, because they were going to take the existing business world head-on, right out of the gate.

When the Internet start-up had capital, it could commission the best design practitioners. Whether the start-up made the decisions about the role design would play or left those decisions to the designer depended largely on the applied experience of the executive team. When the start-up had little capital, it usually tried to cherry-pick where and how design would be applied to the problem (often to the warnings and consternation of the designers). And when the nature of the technology or business model was so new, in many cases all the design effort was focused on convincing investors—as opposed to end customers—that this was something noteworthy to engage with or that not engaging would mean missing out on fantastic future value.

The shifts in the economy and the change brought about by network computing fueled financial interest in new business models. Design was thriving. During the second half of the last century and continuing onward, there would be a proliferation and diversification of design services. With each new branch in the channels used to reach the market and with each new technology, there was a richer flow of information between business and customer. Design responded with specialization of services, and business looked to maximize investments by finding the best-in-class to fill specific needs at lowest costs. In many cases there were value-added services that addressed business needs that were not tied to the design process and didn't require a finished design. These services made the implementation of the design easier by taking off-the-shelf approaches and making minor, superficial changes to make the output seem more "bespoke," or they assisted in the management of the process for which design was commissioned.

Although business has benefited from the changes brought about by technology, technology is changing the nature of business and the relationship between business and customer. Brands are no longer based on a one-way broadcast and reaffirmation of belief systems, and to a great degree, they are defined as much by the customer as by the business. Technology is rapidly changing the entire product/service life cycle, and as Chris Anderson points out in *Makers*, desktop production combined with the Internet's ability to collapse the idea-to-market telescope might just usher in a new industrial revolution that swings control back to the maker/designer.[18]

Implications

What we're trying to illustrate throughout this chapter is that there is a substantial difference between a maker/designer and a business that has taken on the making and designing of a product or service. This split becomes more structurally ingrained when design is also used to build beliefs and demand for value that is not experientially validated through the products or services it represents. And finally, as the touch points that operate between a business and its customers proliferate, design begins to specialize and to provide new value-added design services aimed at making the customer's life easier.

This creates one challenge that is of particular interest to us because it effectively ensures that the current relationship between business and design continues on the present course, a course that we believe should be reexamined. This is what we describe as a method of self-justifying a position of authority. Essentially it operates as follows: When a problem is poorly framed and presented for design to solve in a way that limits design's ability to solve the problem correctly, an ineffective solution reaffirms that design is not in a position to guarantee results and that it's perhaps a subjective endeavor best managed by business. If an effective solution is delivered, it's simply proof that the business has chosen the right designer because business is a better arbiter of what design can do.

Buyers of design services want to see that those they hire can help them be successful. Because most design service providers live and die by the success of the work they do for their clients, it puts the designer at risk of doing a lot of work that may not get leveraged in the future. When your portfolio is filled with projects for companies that went out of business, it's hard to get hired, even if you were just following the clients' orders.

Although we're pointing out the inefficiencies in the way that business and design are now working together, we should be honest and acknowledge that we, and the design industry in general, have benefited a lot from these developments. There are many buyers of design services, and their needs continue to increase and change. We would not be in business today if the circumstances hadn't played out as they have. But what we continue to see is that although this may have benefited us, the same dynamic seems to be working against business. Design should be able to help business identify, create, and deliver more value to their customers. We also believe that this view of the world is useful for businesses, for practitioners delivering design services, and for maker/designers, whether they are part of a start-up or simply an entrepreneur with a 3D printer and a network connection to the market.

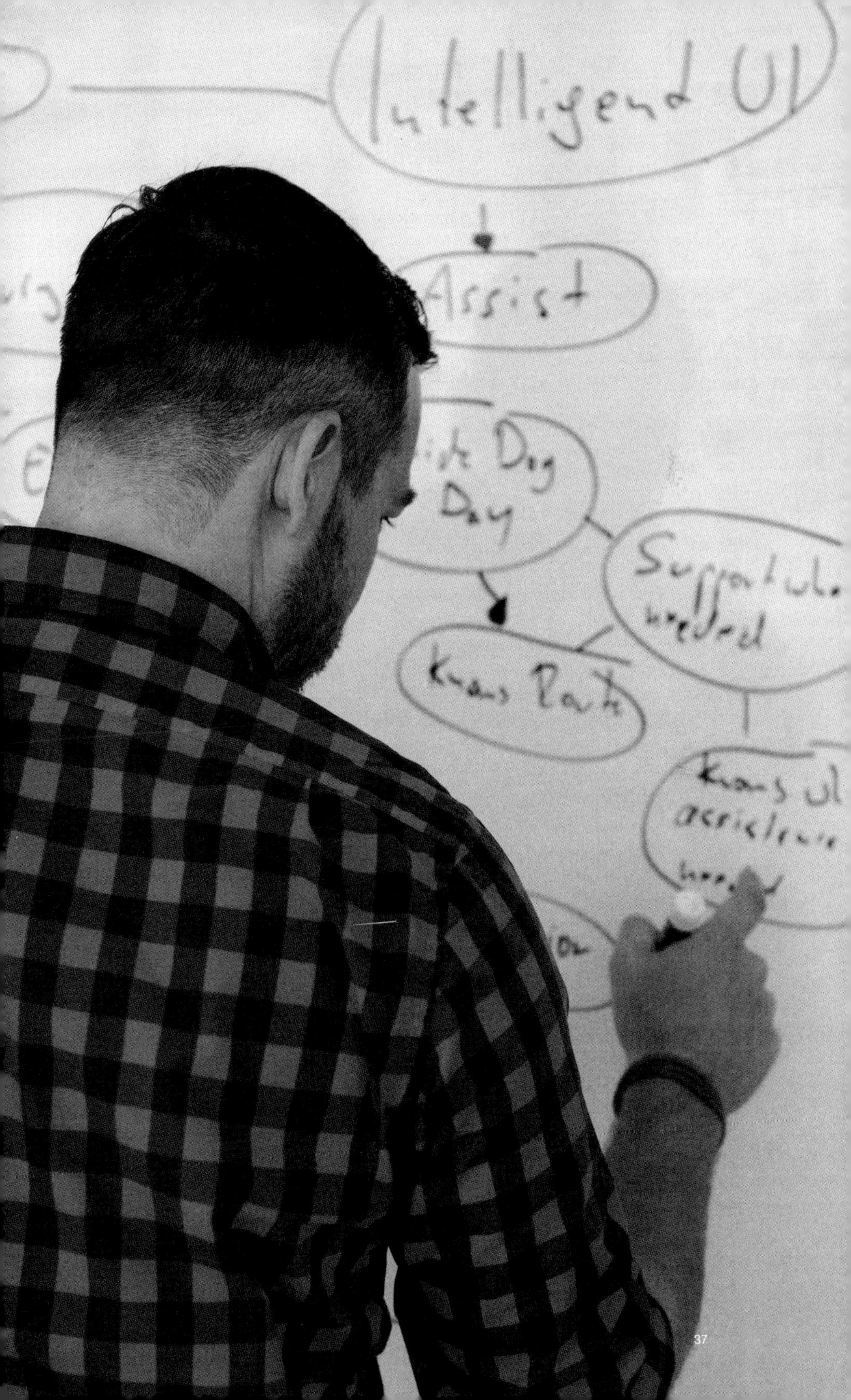
Intelligend UI
Assist

2

Thinking about Business

"When my information changes,
I alter my conclusions.
What do you do, sir?"

—John Maynard Keynes[1]

Variations of this quote have been attributed to different people over the years—Keynes, Winston Churchill, Paul Samuelson—but regardless of who said it, it does illustrate two worthwhile points. The first is literal: No cows should be sacred, and it's good to challenge your own position. Be open to the idea that what you're seeing may be slow change and not stasis. The second is contextual: Despite advances in access to information (such as provided by Google), we can't always be sure we have the facts right. We can't even be 100 percent sure of who said what, as is the case with this oft-cited quote.

We would like to think that Keynes was intuitively familiar with the underlying concept of shifting baseline syndrome, because in *The General Theory of Employment, Interest and Money* (1936), he wrote, "The difficulty lies, not in the new ideas, but in escaping from the old ones, which ramify, for those brought up as most of us have been, into every corner of our minds."[2] We would also like to think that we can convince a good portion of readers to come to the conclusion that things have changed and business is probably not using design as effectively as it could.

We have suggested that design is a natural aptitude, an effective way for humans to approach the world, and that this has probably helped us survive as a species. And, throughout much of our history, what we now think of as design could have been efficiently delivered by the maker/designer. We have moved from centuries of a maker/designer model to one where business now sits between making and design. In this position, it is business that effectively decides how making and design are brought together and what criteria should be used to define and evaluate their output.

Although we believe that business and design have both benefited from this relatively recent transition away from integrated maker/designer, it's probably not the right relationship moving forward. What we are proposing in regard to experience design requires business and design to consider that the relationship between the two, as we know it now, is not the best it could be and that adopting new ways of framing problems and working together could produce a better future.

Let's face it: The current situation creates inefficiencies. This has a lot to do with how businesses manage themselves (developing advantage by maximizing efficiency and reducing costs) and by extension how they manage the split between maker and designer. The very circumstances that allow business to exist in this state—the ability to use consumerism to extract profits from the process of bringing production and design together in certain managed ways—also creates a situation in which mistakes in meeting consumers' expectations can be costly. The ways that business engages design are often driven more by efficiencies of business management or a given company's culture, as opposed to what creates the most value for the customer over time. And the pressures on business brought about by technology narrow the window of opportunity for getting it right. This is compounded by the increasing challenge that technology poses for business in that many of the circumstances now affecting them are outside of their control.

In this chapter we look at the relationship of business and value, how this plays into business's current approach to design, and what factors help drive change for business. We believe that reexamining the relationship between business and design is the best approach for dealing with the pressures now being faced by business and that experience design is a good foundation for reassessing how the two can play off each other's strengths.

The view we are putting forth is fairly pragmatic and based largely on observation and common sense. Although we think it's interesting to ponder how the overall thesis of this book would change how businesses approach strategy, our real objective is to start conversations that make it more productive for business and design to work together. As Arthur Schopenhauer wrote in the opening of *The Art of Always Being Right*[3]:

> We should in every debate have no other aim than the discovery of truth; we should not in the least care whether the truth proved to be in favour of the opinion we had begun expressing, or the opinion of our adversary.

Customer Value and the Goal of Business

We started the Introduction to this book by asking how a business stays in business and suggested that the answer is by creating value (and selling it for less than it originally costs to create). Our answer posed three levels of value: tangible, intangible, and aspirational. What's missing is a description of how that value is identified, created, and delivered to customers.

It's also worth noting that the perception of value is different for business buyers (in business-to-business [B2B] environments) and general consumers (in business-to-consumer [B2C] environments). This difference is especially important at a tactical level (tactics that work well in one case might not be as effective in another). We believe that the general overview we have taken, the current state, and our proposal of experience design is universal for both B2B and B2C companies and, in fact, would provide a much better framework for designing value in the more complex but increasingly common business-to-business-to-consumer (B2B2C) model, where a business sells both to other businesses and consumers.

There have been many attempts to define value in terms of products versus services. We propose a set of definitions below that we will use as we discuss experience design.

> Consumer: Someone who has and demonstrates the capacity to buy products and services from businesses. A consumer becomes a customer of a business when he or she considers buying products or services from that business.

> Customer: A buyer (and potential buyer) of a specific product or service provided by a specific business. A customer's behavior may reflect his or her role as customer in a given situation, and the larger trends in consumer behavior.

> Product: Something that is paid for once, becoming the property of the buyer, and that delivers some form of value or utility without mediation by anyone other than the end user. The cost of a product can be amortized over the useful life of the product. In some cases this value extends well beyond the breakeven point, but this is never guaranteed. When it does, it's generally good for business.

> Products can become service channels when they are able to provide information or access to a service. In some cases this channel is used by other businesses that may or may not have a financial relationship with the

business that makes and sells the product. In some cases, the predominant value of the product is as a service delivery channel.

Service: A service is something that must be paid for on an ongoing basis (never becoming the property of the buyer). It delivers some form of value or utility to a user but requires the direct support or mediation of another (either the seller, a partner to the seller, or someone commissioned by the buyer of the service). The cost of a service can never be amortized because you are essentially always paying for the right or access to use it, whether you actually use it or not.

Because of the relationship between value and intermediaries in a service, the economics of securing all the necessary components in advance of use would be prohibitive for any single buyer. Or, as in many cases, a component of the value or utility is based on another service, which means that the total service can never fully become the property of a single customer.

Services can be bundled together with other services, often from different businesses (providers). Services can use products as channels for reaching and engaging customers. Many services would be of no value to a given customer if the products through which they are delivered were not already owned by that customer. In some cases services subsidize the cost of these products for the consumer. Because it is common for the product to be made and sold by someone other than the service provider, services may have different characteristics (and value propositions) depending on which products they are delivered through.

Solution: A combination of products and/or services that can be combined and modified to provide specific, multistage value. Some solutions can be created or modified by customers, whereas others require professional services of some kind.

Once someone has bought a product, the gap between the product value and his or her needs becomes the buyer's responsibility. When someone buys a service, the gap between the service value and his or her needs is still the buyer's responsibility, but one way the buyer can deal with this is by discontinuing the service. With a solution, the gap between value and need is dynamic and can be affected by changing or changes to the components.

These ways of looking at value generally map to the core touch points that any business uses to provide value for its customers. These exist within a larger set of touch points that are used to communicate and transact with customers. Interestingly, how you look at these touch points of value—what's important and why—depends on what your background and current role is (business decision maker versus maker versus designer). Although we may all agree in principle that these definitions are useful, what a businessperson thinks is important might be very different from what a maker or designer deems most important. And this is natural, so it's to be expected.

Howard Gardner is someone who believes that there is not one single model of human intelligence that operates in each of us. In addition to being a prolific writer, Gardner who also happens to be a developmental psychologist and the John H. and Elisabeth A. Hobbs Professor of Cognition **and Education at the Harvard Graduate**

School of Education. Many of his books are about his (and others') emerging theories connecting psychology, biology, and neuroscience with the purpose of understanding human intelligence. A main theme in his work is that there are multiple intelligences at work in the human mind that give rise to the variety of capabilities we see and commonly think of as intelligence.[4] He also proposes that this is a good thing, because it helps provide a level of robustness for intelligence across the species.

For those of us who often find ourselves at the table with business and design, this idea of multiple intelligences is probably nothing new. We have all heard business-minded people refer to some aspect of the problem they are trying to solve to be outside of their capabilities and that they are looking to "you creative types who know how to solve these things." Conversely, we have often heard designers say that it's not their job to figure out the business model or "determine what KPIs [key performance indicators] are relevant and what their measurement would mean." It's quite easy to inadvertently become biased and think that another possesses a level of capability that is greater than ours, especially when it's reinforced within a more formal set of role and relationship definitions and expectations. The downside to this kind of thinking is closing our minds to the parts of a problem that we aren't as comfortable solving.

Under the maker/designer model, an efficient approach to creating value for many centuries, the decisions about what value was in a given situation were probably envisioned from one point of view. There weren't a lot of options (knowledge, technology, money) for the maker/designer in the creation of value. Given that, it's likely that the spectrum of value demanded by the customer (and the need to explore this and provide a highly differentiated offering) was also relatively low. Essentially, there was a more single-minded view of how production and design were combined to create something of value.

It's no stretch of the imagination to see that if the mind-set determining what and how to create value for customers is now based more on managing processes and optimizing costs and efficiencies, then a different kind of prioritization of objectives arises that may subordinate those of either the maker or the designer. This will also affect how people within a business develop strategies for identifying and accomplishing goals. Considering this, what would be an appropriate model for having a single-minded approach to how business and design join forces to create value?

Michael Porter, once the guru of business strategy (perhaps now a more controversial figure, as some of his assumptions have recently been challenged[5]), viewed competition as the key element of looking at business strategy. His views on competition and what's important from a competitive perspective will make sense to most people, because they align with an intuitive sense of a business's goals as being the creation and delivery of value.

In *HBR's 10 Must Reads on Strategy*, Porter provided an answer to the question "What is strategy?" He writes[6]:

> To outperform rivals: [business] must deliver greater value to customers or create comparable value at a lower cost, or do both. Overall advantage or disadvantage results from all a company's activity, not only a few. The myriad activities that go into creating, producing, selling, and delivering a product or service are the basic units of competitive advantage. . . .

Strategy requires you to make trade-offs in competing—to choose what not to do. Strategy involves creating "fit" among a company's activities.

Critics of Porter are also largely critics of this view and point out that competition as strategy essentially assumes a zero-sum game, one in which there has to be a loser and a winner. These counterviews would suggest that an ecosystem model is more accurate—that one doesn't necessarily need a rival to go out of business to see some kind of advantage. Often, the focus is moved away from competing with rivals and instead looks at creating value for the customer.

It's interesting to reread Porter's description of strategy but replace *competing* and *competitive advantage* with *creating value for your customers*. Certainly Porter understands the basic role of value, as he is essentially saying that's where it all starts. We suggest that this replacement is crucial to the future of the business and design relationship and is a core component of our approach to experience design. It's also worth pointing out that Porter believes it is important to look at all activities and how they fit together. Keeping value for your customer and ensuring coherency across all activities are the foundations of the approach to experience design that we propose in this book.

One term that has become synonymous with competition in many business minds, or at least in the minds of much of the business press over the past decade, is *innovation*. We will discuss innovation in the next chapter, but it's useful to briefly raise a point here, as it ties into how businesses tend to approach customer value (and we are assuming that most businesses have chosen innovation as their way of competing, similar to Porter's original definition of *strategy*).

Ron Adner has made a major contribution to understanding innovation in a book called *The Wide Lens*. The basic thesis is that innovation doesn't happen in a vacuum and that for any innovation to work, there is a network of players and considerations that must be looked at and managed. One of the key points, though, is that tied to the innovation mind-set is the assumption that business is in a position to accurately define what value is. In many cases the definitions are not correct. Adner's point is an important one[7]:

> We all know that a natural tension exists between those selling a product and their target buyers. At its root is a misunderstanding over the notion of value—the balance between costs and benefits. Although both innovators and consumers use the terms "cost" and "benefit" to describe the way they think about value, they think about those terms in very different ways.

Adner says that missing this difference in perspective is a "recipe for disaster" and clarifies how this difference in views comes about, arguing that it largely revolves around whether or not the value is truly a benefit.

Adner goes on to say[8]:

> Innovators think about these benefits in terms of what their product actually provides—the absolute benefit delivered to the customer. But customers think about benefits in terms of added value—the relative benefit delivered by the product compared to the available alternatives.

Considering what alternatives exist for the customer should include the option of not buying anything or making do with what they currently have (Porter does consider this in his 5 Forces model of competition). Adner continues to point out how the difference in benefit is compounded by the different perceptions of cost[9]:

> Innovators tend to think of the price they charge for their innovation as the determinant of customer cost, customers conceive of cost in terms of that price plus all the other changes they need to undertake in order to use the innovation (beyond the initial outlay, the cost of retraining, equipment upgrades, etc.). While innovators tend to focus on delivering an offer whose absolute benefits exceed the purchase price, adoption happens only if the customer sees a clear surplus. That is, the relative benefits must exceed the total cost.

If we change this view slightly and consider that rather than innovations (new offers) we are looking at existing offers targeted at new customers or at superficial improvements (for example, the New and Improved! messaging on the packaging) targeted at existing customers, we would suggest that Adner's description is still accurate. In fact, this describes how a lot of us look at making decisions regarding what to buy and from whom, not just how we look at innovations.

So how does business do a better job of identifying the true benefit to the customer? How should decisions be made about which trade-offs in cost versus value need to be made?

In the book *Different: Escaping the Competitive Herd*, Harvard Business School professor of marketing Youngme Moon talks about how companies try to differentiate themselves to build stronger demand and more valuable relationships with customers. What she points out is that many of the efforts employed by businesses are short lived, have a high cost, and don't really sway consumers' minds. It's a brinkmanship model in which any move by one competitor is eventually adopted by the other regardless of costs and longer-term benefits. Consumers are happy to take advantage of the additional value, but because it's not exclusive, it doesn't drive loyalty. Moon's point is that this route of competing for customers, largely by mimicking the competition, is not sustainable and that it may be more effective to determine what a business does best and what customers value the most, and in turn focus on making that value exchange as strong as possible.[10]

We like to think that all businesses, especially our clients, realize the importance of creating value for customers. But we do see that in many cases, this becomes a lesser priority when leaders are looking at issues, initiatives, and future plans. Why is it that this important point often fades or is present but in an extremely abstract way that is difficult to put into action?

The Challenges of Identifying, Creating, and Delivering Value

In addition to managing operations in a cost-effective way, business also needs to ensure that customers are receiving value in ways that they *agree* are valuable. Competition will always exist, and figuring out how to do all of this in a way that differentiates you from rivals while building loyalty with customers is the goal.

One of the key takeaways is understanding value and making sure that the business and customer sides of the equation balance. This is one area where design can play an important role, if only to structure the problem in such a way that helps customers realize the value in a way that is apparent and realistic. Of course, value, like beauty, is in the eyes of the beholder. One way to make sure that you deliver the right balance of value is to think like the "beholder."

In the early days of the Internet phenomenon, one challenge was helping provide context for what a user was looking at, what it meant, and what he or she could do, or was supposed to do, at any given point. During this phase of the Web's development, the hyperlink, or text-link (blue type with the line underneath), as a way to navigate through information was a new concept for many users. The idea that someone had to understand the purpose and implications of these links led to the coining of the term *cognitive overhead*: the effort of understanding the purpose and implication of all that blue text.

There is a story about a high-powered executive; a partner in one of the big five consulting companies who never used his computer. He had his administrative assistant do everything, including reading his e-mail, writing e-mail on his behalf, and so on; essentially, this partner knew what the computer did but didn't find it valuable enough to bother to learn to use it. According to the story, another partner informed the first one that all of the SEC filings that companies were legally required to provide were available online in a database called EDGAR. The Luddite partner then became very adept at using the computer because access to this information was extremely valuable to his job.[11]

What works about this story is that it perfectly illustrates how value works. People will use a product or service, despite difficulty, if they perceive it provides enough value. We call this concept the cognitive overhead rule and often use it in pitches and in projects, writing it as the ratio:

Perceived value / cognitive overhead

We say that if the result is less than 1 (overhead greater than value), there would be a problem and the product or service won't be successful. Conversely, a result greater than 1 would be much better. We also point out that there are two ways to approach the problem. One is to reduce the cognitive overhead through design; the other is to make sure the value is very high by making sure you solved a customer's real need (again, through design). Often, we say looking to do both was the best bet.

We propose updating this model and applying it to the totality of things a business does on behalf of the customer and would write it as follows:

Perceived value of what has been provided by business /
efforts a customer has to make on his or her own behalf to receive full value

What might be obvious to many readers is that this ratio is likely to change over time. That change is going to determine the context in which the value/effort ratio is being played out. There's a difference between the first time a customer uses a product or service and the hundredth time. There is a difference between what a customer expects based on advertising and marketing versus what that person actually experiences. There is a difference between how someone might expect to be treated the first time he or she does business with you versus after having paid you lots of money. And there is a difference in what satisfies a customer's needs when that person is relaxed and has time to spare versus when that person is under pressure and has other things that require his or her attention.

We think that experience design means factoring time into every decision and understanding what the relevant vectors of time are for any given stage or touch point of the customer experience. With this view in mind, we would make one final change to this model and write it as:

$$\text{Perceived Value} = \frac{\left(\begin{array}{c} \text{What has been done or} \\ \text{provided by a business} \end{array} \right) - \left[\left(\begin{array}{c} \text{Customer} \\ \text{needs} \end{array} \right) \times \left(\begin{array}{c} \text{Customer} \\ \text{expectations} \end{array} \right) \right]}{\text{Customer context}}$$

Of course, these are not real equations; you can't plug data or metrics into them and produce a quantitative answer. But they are useful when looking at any given project or customer touch point. We will go into more detail about how this approach works in the next few chapters. The important point for now is to begin to think about what's going on over time with the customer, the customer's experience around a product or service, and the overall relationship with the business. The goal of business's use of design (both process and outcome) is to ensure as much seamless experience of value as possible for the customer in order to keep the customer engaged.

The challenge for both business and design is to prevent the value from becoming overly fragmented or faceted to the point where the customer is no longer engaged, or worse, sees no value in further engagement.

The Origins of Faceted Value

As we mentioned before, anyone who has sat at the same table alongside business and design has probably experienced people who seem more business-minded and others who are more design-minded. We believe that they collaborate most efficiently when each mind-set understands—and values—the importance of what the other brings to the table. This means that the maker/designer represents the thinking about what the customer would really find valuable and how to enhance its value, and the business-minded person thinks about how to manage the creation and delivery of value to the market in the most efficient manner possible to allow the business and design to make a living together.

In such a scenario, the two sides would have to work with each other to discuss which trade-offs create the most viable model of meeting each other's goals. They would then be able to make iterative adjustments to their model as they actually begin to implement it.

In discussing the difference between how humans have evolved toolmaking capabilities and how this differs from nonhumans, Frank Wilson introduces the terms *polypod* and *polylith* to describe two different kinds of things that can be made by animals[12]:

> Two terms make the distinction clear. The first term, "lith" refers to any subunit of a tool (or any other manufactured object), called a "polylith," whose components are mechanically joined. The second term, "pod," refers to the subunits of a multiple-unit object or structure, called a "polypod," which depends on gravity for its stability.

Both humans and nonhuman primates can make polypods. . . . A polylith, by contrast, is an object consisting of any number of joined units, or sub assemblies, that can be freely rotated without disturbing the structural or functional integrity of the object.

We like this as an analogy for creating value through design. It's relatively easy to create points of value, specific instances in which all the requirements and options can clearly be analyzed. But creating more complex forms of value isn't simply aggregating specific components and hoping that they work well together. This is a polypod approach to complex value. On first blush, it looks good, but with a little stress, it falls apart into separate and less useful unintegrated components. It would seem that making sure that components of value are more integrated and more "polylithic" would be good for both business and customer (and for a solution to be valuable, it needs to maintain integration even while components change). There are many challenges with this way of going about things, at least with regard to how design can help.

This brings us to the question of how business is using design to create value for customers. From our experience, the role of "arbiter of value" now sits with business (that is, the decision of what is made, how it's made, for whom, and how design is leveraged). When decisions made by this authority are primarily concerned with efficiency, cost, and competition or when they are constrained in terms of input of information and scope of effect (within a limited portion of the business), the results can be problematic. Although the business may see all the decisions as being the best, given objectives and limitations, the outside world may have a different view. Gaps and inconsistencies in thinking and planning are mostly apparent to customers; their experience is much bumpier and less satisfying than it could be. In some cases, there may not even be a business owner to whom one can take an issue because it arose from two different areas of the company that aren't collaborating well enough, each believing that they have done their job adequately.

Without intending to, business risks creating a fragmented view of the overall problem they are setting out to solve: creating value for the customer. Much of the inefficiency here is a result of the way in which the business is organized and how this determines where decision making is made and who is delivering which parts of the overall value of design.

Businesses tend to approach the creation of value by using design (process and outcome) in two ways. The first is the making/process side of design as it relates to core development processes for the value of the products and services. This is often performed by employees within internal business units. The reasons for having these skills in-house are to have direct access to the knowledge of the makers and to develop and protect the intellectual property that constitutes parts of their core competence and competitive strategy. In this role, the processes and decisions are largely managed with a focus on functional utility and financial efficiency.

The second way business uses design is in the packaging and management of demand generation and support of product or service use, with a focus on driving transactions (attractiveness and initial desirability). In larger enterprises this is often managed by the marketing function.

Many smaller businesses can't afford to have makers or designers on staff, or the scale or required expertise for a project exceeds in-house design capabilities. In these cases, businesses turn to external design agencies both for product/service and nonproduct/nonservice design needs. Many larger firms have entire procurement departments to manage the process of working with partners. In either case, there is often a different kind of partner used for production-related design as opposed to marketing/selling-related design.

Providing design services is our business; we are very thankful that our clients decide to use our services. That being said, we do need to point out several challenges when businesses decide to call all the shots when engaging outside designers. The first is that outside agencies have evolved to largely be a set of skills looking for a problem. From this context, it's business that decides when design should be brought to the table and for what reason. Although good designers will have an appetite for opening a problem up and trying to understand all of the upstream and downstream relationships that need to be considered, it's usually business deciding what objectives design should accomplish. This is often because the problem is considered to be well understood by business, so the budget, time frame, and scope are often determined before engaging design resources.

If the decision to use an external design source comes from within a department, this can lead to an isolation of the project down to a very specific and bounded ask. Any request for services made by a buyer in this case requires a response that will convince that buyer that the design agency can solve that specific kind of problem in the way it has been posed, in a highly cost-efficient manner (without sacrificing quality), even if such an approach is not in the best interest of the customer or the business as a whole.

Often, the decision-making criteria for whom to work with begins by looking at the category of outputs a design firm has previously worked on, choosing the best and budget-aligned options by evaluating how closely the previous outputs match what the business is looking to do, and then discussing what processes were involved and why.

From the external partner perspective, there is little opportunity to point out flaws or risks. The logic of these kinds of assignments can seem dubious, as the problem definition and constraints may preclude meeting the objectives in a way that creates real value for the business (or its customers). This leads to the regrettable attitude by the external team that they are "putting lipstick on a pig"—that what they are doing doesn't matter and can't really add value. Whether or not this is true is less important than the fact that a team that doesn't believe they can make an impact is less likely to try and therefore less likely to succeed. The opposite can also happen, leading to both sides being extremely happy with the outcome, not realizing that there were bigger implications that were missed. Although everyone walks away satisfied, the outcome fails to move the needle because it didn't integrate effectively into the overall delivery of value to the customer.

Another problem can arise when divisions within the company prevent the correct development of problem focus. In such cases, key inputs are not factored in and important stakeholders are not included (by intent or oversight). It's not uncommon to see functional units battle regarding design decisions. We've been in many situations where marketing believed that certain approaches and objectives for design made sense, but the product team disagreed. In several cases, because product was more tied to revenue (with marketing being a cost center), the product point of view won, as marketing was afraid that executive management would side with revenue over any other consideration.

We have also seen the opposite, where marketing was supporting business development and features were determined to be needed not because the customers demanded them but because marketing or business development had promised other partners (such as strategic partners, channel partners, distributors, etc.) that they'd be included. We have seen marketing hire design for a specific purpose and then a product group—liking the outcome—hire its own agency to produce the same thing. In this case, because the knowledge and expertise of the two firms providing design services were very different, the final "products" were very different. This left the product team unable to deliver the value to customers in the way that they had hoped.

Design's ability to solve the kinds of problems that left unaddressed can undermine value for customers is limited if a business makes all the decisions about how and when to apply design skills. At the same time, it's not efficient to have design teams involved in every aspect of business decision making. Experience design can help to alleviate this situation by providing a more design-centric framework for business planners to work from, and helping business integrate specific areas of design strategy and expertise during planning processes. As the need to react to change increases, this kind of efficiency is going to be more and more important.

3

Thinking about Change

Ancient peoples believed that
time was cyclic in character . . .
We, on the other hand, habitually
think of time as something that
stretches in a straight line into
the past and future . . .
The linear concept of time has had
profound effects on Western thought.
Without it, it would be difficult to
conceive of the idea of progress.

—Robert Morris, as quoted by Stephen Jay Gould in *Time's Arrow, Time's Cycle*[1]

The Implication of Time

Over the course of its lifetime, a business will have varying design needs. Too often, design is focused within a narrow sliver of time, compared with the life of the business, and the relationship a customer may have with the business. As a result, design is often deemed necessary only at certain stages, and once these have been completed, it is as if what has been created will suffice forever and never needs to be revisited.

The "foundation" for many businesses is their brand. Brand means many things to many people, but for most modern businesses, it provides several basic requirements: what the company is called and what its identity (logo or trademark) looks like, its mission and vision, and often its values and positioning. Because these are things that don't need to change frequently (except when a major change has occurred, such as a substantial shift in the offering, a major gaffe in performance or behavior, or the hiring of a new chief marketing officer [CMO]), this is an area that rarely gets attention from design. There are pragmatic reasons for not changing the brand frequently, such as brand equity, awareness, and costs of implementation. There are other aspects of the brand that can be explored on an ongoing basis that don't require these kinds of investments or risks.

The next area where design plays a role is in the products or services of a company. As we've mentioned, many of the needs here relate to the make/process side of design and may be brought in-house. In cases in which the scale of the effort or the nature of the expertise requires it, outside partners may be brought in. But in either case, the investments made for products and services are expected to provide returns over time. So products and services remain relatively stable once they are designed and go through ordered and planned design evolution (often with small and incremental changes). Part of this also relates to how much value the customer gets from a product or service and how much of this value is based on the product remaining the same versus changing. As such, products and services often get the most attention from design when they are first being developed. One of the objectives of experience design is to try to identify what kind of future variations might make sense and be valuable to customers so that product can plan for them. It's a lot easier to implement something later that you had planned on than to implement something you hadn't.

Finally, design is used in the communications and interactions with customers. Because much of this falls into marketing, advertising, sales, or customer support, these design efforts are thought of as expenses. These areas are often the ones that change the most frequently.

The outcome of this process of employing design is that design may be engaged the most for work in areas where the business engages with the customer but provides the least value. What design is asked to create is really the window dressings and not the core value that's identified, created, and delivered to the customer. Business should not expect this type of design to create value for the customer, or more specifically, for design to be able to make up for a lack of value in the core definition of the product or service. At best, design can make certain aspects of the product or service easier to use, make information more accessible, or accentuate the presentation of messaging to stimulate response, but none of this is creating real value for the businesses' customers. And at worst, it is papering over significant gaps in value. In the coming chapters we will show how experience design can help to change this by looking at how experiences that engage customers in the right way can do double duty of helping prime the sales funnel while also setting up customer value (in some cases even before the customer decides to buy).

Another by-product of this approach to managing design over time is that the design that goes into things such as the brand or formative product/service design may be very disconnected from the design with which the customers engage. Not only was it created at a different point in time but often it was created by different people with different skills and expertise for different facets of the problem. In many cases there is no thread that integrates the design throughout. Take this simple test: Get a copy of your company's brand guidelines. Now look up how the design of the brand should affect the design of the product. If you're lucky, it will tell you which form of the logo should be used and what colors the product should be. But that's only if you're lucky. Even then, it's highly unlikely that the guidelines would cover any aspect of what kind of value the product should deliver or how it should deliver it.

Two additional aspects of time that affect how business and design collaborate should also be considered. The first aspect worth looking at is where business is focused when employing design. Often, there is the propensity for business to think upstream. In laying out where design sits, where it is used by business, and the frequency with which design attention is applied, we are using an implicit assumption on the part of how business thinks. This is an assumption we have seen our more informed clients raise as an issue within their own approach to customers. Simply put, it's a tendency to focus on the presales side of the customer relationship.

When attempts to produce innovation are made through research and development and you invest in converting these ideas into products and services, it's natural to want to increase the odds of success by creating as much demand as possible and making the transaction as efficient as possible. After that you can see the revenue that will determine if you are going to be successful or not. But once the cycle has been completed, the next cycle already has to have started, working to continually produce the returns and level of growth that stakeholders are expecting. Customer support and relationship management are becoming increasingly important, but currently these are more process-driven and design's role is minimized. Much of the efforts here are taken to prime the pump for the next cycle.

Ideally, a customer will spend more time using your product or service than he or she will spend in the sales funnel. It seems somewhat shortsighted for business to not focus as much on post-sales engagement and value. If it's easier to sell to existing customers than new customers, why are customers largely left on their own navigating through all the facets of value, including trying to make your product or service work for them? Why do most businesses contact existing customers only to try to sell more and not engage them around how they are getting existing value? Why doesn't a business plan for proactive engagement when a customer discontinues use of a product or service the business has been providing?

The second important aspect of time is its impact on customer value given the nature of technology and the products and services it enables. In the first chapter, we talked about the new area of design that computing and network technologies required: interaction design. One of the fundamental aspects of this area of design is what happens over time—how a product or service needs to function (and respond) as a customer engages with it. Many of the issues that design considers when looking at products and services this way are related to different areas of the business (information technology [IT], accounts and finance, other products and services, etc.).

As we pointed out when discussing how business uses design, often the scope of a problem is constrained or stakeholders are not represented. Many of the design issues that arise have no associated final decision maker. The decision of one stakeholder can be at odds with the goals of another, or choices in one area can have a negative impact for a completely different product or service. The result is that many decisions may not be made or they get made with an incorrect understanding of their impact. Not only can these be costly to correct, but they can also remain unseen or unacknowledged until discovered by a customer. The nature of what is being designed may tax businesses' ability to understand how to evaluate design criteria. In many situations, interaction design is dealing with representing a task (in processes and flows) that has no preexisting analogy or counterpart in the physical or cognitive world of the customer. The key criteria that design should be accounting for are ones that help drive engagement. In other words, does the process provide enough value to customers to make them want to continue to use it?

Technology also opens up interactive (bidirectional) channels between a business and a customer. In some cases there is considerable latency, but in others the nature of the channel is inherently more responsive, so people expect some reaction (or proactivity). From a business perspective, this means several things: Find the ways in which a customer's engagement can be used to create value for the business and explore how different forms and means of engagement can be used to build higher lifetime value from each customer.

One of the key questions facing businesses today is: Who is responsible for understanding the interdependencies across all of the areas in which design is applied, and how are they evaluating the real impact—on the customer and the business—of all of the design decisions being made? We believe that business should be taking a more holistic look at customer value across the customer experience. But the challenge of managing an ongoing experience that engages people around value is getting more difficult. This is one of the prime drivers for the model of experience design we propose in the next few chapters. What we think is missing is a unified framework for creating value for customers based on a given business, brand, and offering.

We also believe that not shifting their thinking will lead to businesses finding out the hard way that the ways of doing things in the past needs to change, largely because businesses aren't in control of the larger world in which their value exists.

Technology and the Evolution of Value

Imagine arriving at an airport and stepping off a plane in the late evening. You aren't arriving home but rather preparing to continue your travels by car. Having secured a reservation when you originally made your travel plans, you follow the signs to the rental car counter. The cordoning ribbons guide you to a spot where you will wait for the next available customer service associate. You notice that there are four people ahead of you and two customer service agents already working with customers. No worries; you have time. But time goes by and more people join the line behind you. The customer service associates are still engaged with the customers they had when you first got in line. Each customer seems to have some kind of situation or question that requires an additional conversation and review of options.

Time passes, and you begin to wonder how long you have been waiting. About 15 minutes have elapsed. Other agents appear, walk up to computers, seem to do something, and then walk off and disappear behind closed doors. Finally, both of the agents free up, and there are now only two people standing between you, your car, and forward progress. Things seem to move a little faster now, and the two people in front of you are being served. But when one is finished and you think it's your turn, the customer service agent gets up and disappears behind the closed doors in back. Those behind you in line are expressing their exasperation. Finally, after waiting for close to 25 minutes, more associates appear, and quickly you are on your way. Of course, there is still one more surprise. The type of car you had reserved and were promised by the agent is not available on the lot. By this time, it's very late in the evening, and with no other options, you have to take what they give you.

Throughout all of this, you are analyzing the situation, looking at everything that the car rental company could be doing differently, and comparing it in your mind to a very different experience—on-demand car rental (such as Zipcar). You realize that the Zipcar experience puts the responsibility on you to arrange everything—but that's the advantage: You are in complete control, and as such you can make the process as efficient as you would like. You also vow to never rent again from the rental company you have just used, and consider how you will potentially look to something like Zipcar for future needs.

What is interesting about this example is that the difference between the customer experience and the level of satisfaction perceived are dramatically different for what is essentially a similar service. What is the difference, and why would a company choose one kind of experience over the other? One of the major reasons is the role of technology.

The customer service model used by the rental car company is one that has been around for years and is based on the need for human to be an intermediary in delivering a service. The on-demand car rental model has benefited from a shift in technology that makes it very easy to have most of the functions of the intermediary made possible by automated systems. The options available to the end customer can be presented directly to the customer, wherever and whenever is most convenient.

Many rental car companies have begun to take advantage of this shift, but mostly for their preferred customers. What this story represents is a move toward what's possible, what's efficient, and what will eventually be a more appealing and satisfying experience for consumers. All of this is made possible by a large-scale shift in technologies, as opposed to an option that was available to all when the customer experience models were being developed.

The point is that as technology advances, many things will need to change. Although many of our clients have been most affected by changes in information and communication technologies, technology change is happening everywhere in every industry and every sector. Because consumers cross industry segments, the changes and expectations of one industry can affect those in other industries who have not yet seen the need or advantage to question the status quo.

Simply put, changes in technology affect value—its identification, creation, delivery, and even perceptions and expectations. This can be a good thing. For instance, digital technology has reduced the cost of production in many instances to the point that after a certain quantity, a product essentially has no cost of production. Because one can now serve customers through many more channels, new services can be developed at a much faster pace, with significantly fewer challenges for reaching consumers.

The shorter-term benefits of technology may also have broader long-term implications that are less beneficial, though. For instance, services that can be delivered by or that rely on information and communication technology have the ability to evolve faster than purely physical products. Most of these services need some artifacts as part of the creation and delivery of value. This creates what we call the product/solution curve. The product/solution curve is based on the progression of value delivered by a product to meet a given use case or need.

As the capabilities of the product features increase, there is a point at which additional utility and value are achieved by adding a service capability to the product. As this is added and a product now becomes a service channel, other services can potentially be combined. If there are other service-enabled products that are compatible and complementary, they can all be used, creating an ecosystem of value. With enough value, this ecosystem becomes a solution that in many cases can make the original use case or need that spawned the product obsolescent. There is no longer a market case for the stand-alone product, and in some cases this even affects the economics of entire industries.

A recent example of this is the iPod. Originally created to solve the problem of transporting and listening to MP3 files that were created when a consumer converted a CD to computer-accessible files, the iPod and its related services and products have eliminated the need to buy CDs (and have shifted consumer behavior away from buying CDs as products to consuming music as a service). Similar shifts have affected other industries and products, with photography being another recent example (shifts from analog to digital to dynamic focal points to self-destructing digital photos and the disappearance of products and companies that have been around for decades).

One of the opportunities that this opens up is a concept we call "the value gap" and an associated concept: "value siphoning". In the value gap concept, customers can't adopt new value as technologies change because they're constrained by their own financial situation and can't or won't invest in the new options. They need to get as much value out of their existing equipment, and in many cases, the provider has already moved on to pushing new options. This leaves customers in a precarious situation. In some cases they may have new needs as a result of their adoption of a new product or service. In some cases the business providing the product or service, having moved on to new offerings, is unable to take advantage of the opportunity and provide the right level of value. Or worse, the original provider didn't anticipate the emerging need and isn't focused on it, but a competitor or new entrant is. This new opportunist is able to "syphon" the enabling value and deliver an additional level, often creating a stronger relationship with the customer than the original business had.

We pointed out earlier that business has often taken a compete-based-on-optimizing-and-efficiency approach to the world. Perhaps this was the intuitive response to dealing with a significant margin between what it cost to produce something and what the market would bear, something that came about during the Industrial Revolution and then was later reinforced through applications of "scientific" approaches to optimization and the management of processes. In such a world, a differentiated product provided a bit of competitive advantage, especially if you could create a demand for that difference in the mind of the consumer. If what your product could provide did really go to "11" (as opposed to 10), you could outsell competitors because they would need to (1) realize why the alternative you provided is desirable, (2) become convinced that they need to adapt/adopt or come up with a better model, (3) develop and deploy it, and (4) have a market reception that's actually sustainable.

If we are now considering the role of services, solutions, and technology in value, this approach would provide little sustainable advantage. The length of product/ service cycles is shortening. To outcompete in this world, one has to come up with a differentiation in value that moves the market and provides an advantage for long enough to pay for the changes involved in creating and delivering it. But as Youngme Moon points out in *Different*,[2] this may not be working anymore. The only real difference between alternatives may be the experience people have. And matching an experience step for step is not rocket science (although managing it across all possible steps and nonlinear variations can be challenging).

So, from our point of view, we believe that things are changing in how businesses successfully identify, create, and deliver value. Some of this is coming about as a result of what business does and how it has been successful in the past. Some of it is because business now has assumed responsibilities it may not be well versed in managing without looking at the world in new ways. And a lot of it is being brought about by changes happening beyond the walls and controls of business, in the general context and environment in which businesses and consumers exist.

For the sake of brevity, we have portrayed a linear and serial transition from the dominance of a maker/designer model to one in which business decides how to manage the duality of design, and we did the same in describing the transition from design being the integration of process and outcome to the growth of formal systems of design that can be used to create value in parallel with, and through incremental additions to, the process of making done by others. We have been fairly linear in our description of how technology shifts value from products to services, but we know that the world is anything but linear, or serial—it's nonlinear and parallel.

When we think of nonlinear, parallel change over time, the example that most readily comes to mind is evolution in the natural world. What makes this model most appealing is that it operates without any assumptions of where things are going, nor does it require a single path of intent for adaptation. It mirrors what we see in the context of products, services, and solutions in a critical way: The environment determines which traits will be the most successful. We believe that the recent changes in technology and markets are beyond any single business's control. What works is largely contingent on being successful for that environment at that time.

Products evolve as a result of changes in context of use, technology for production and delivery of value, and the underlying economics of industries. Services can adapt more readily to change, but they still need to be capable of change. The result is a world in which relentless innovation has become a reality for business—not a choice or a part of the culture but an undeniable reality. If you aren't figuring out new ways to deliver value to your customers, you can rest assured that someone else is. And the economics that make it possible for your business to exist may be changing, perhaps even threatened, by technologies that are just beginning to be explored in a research and development (R&D) department in a different industry.

The Innovation Mirage

The Internet and the promise of a "new economy" that it would usher in were the most talked about topics of the 1990s. Throughout the first decade of this century, the word *innovation* has become the talisman for business. The business press has done all it can to exhaust the topic. Many books have been written about it, and we, ourselves, have even engaged in lively debates at events, with clients, and on projects about whether design is the same as innovation. (It's not.) Everyone is looking for it, and many consultants and agencies from various fields of design are being hired to deliver it.

The more we treat innovation as the next big thing we need to search for, the more we miss the obvious areas where we can innovate. And the likelihood of identifying the next big idea through a focused effort is not reassuringly high. As Scott Berkun puts it in *The Myths of Innovation*[3]:

> Our confidence in innovation approximates a faith; when in doubt, innovate, despite the growing wave of unanswered questions about innovations past.

The number of successful product innovations is low. Ron Adner calls successful innovation the exception and cites the evidence[4]:

> According to surveys by the Product Development and Management Association (PDMA), approximately one out of four new product development efforts ever reach the stage of commercial launch. And even within this highly screened group, 45 percent fail to meet their profit objectives.

Business cannot mandate innovation, nor can it reliably bank on it to simply materialize from within. Michael Mainelli and Ian Harris point out this challenge in their book *The Price of Fish: A New Approach to Wicked Economics and Better Decisions*. In a vein similar to Ron Adner in *The Wide Lens*, Mainelli and Harris suggest that businesses, industry regulators, and governments get themselves in hot water by framing problems too narrowly and then are overly hopeful that innovation will appear to solve the problems, not understanding that innovation itself is a highly unpredictable process.

With regard to innovation there are two sects. In the top-down sect, policy and planning lead to innovation. In the bottom-up sect of wild markets and innovation, you have no idea where the next big idea will come from. Sadly, large numbers of stories show that large companies are not that good at "hard" measurable innovation of the top-down variety. But bottom-up innovation means that corporate headquarters has no idea where the next big idea will emerge.[5]

We propose that, instead of hoping for a miracle of innovation, business rethink innovation. If it is, in fact, now relentless, then it should be part of the process, not a set of special efforts and investments that leaders hope provide an answer. As Adner says, "hope is not a strategy."[6]

We suggest that innovation actually be considered from within the context of the evolution analogy we proposed earlier. We aren't alone in seeing this connection. Mainelli and Harris use the comparison in their book as well. They write[7]:

> There are numerous comparisons to be made between commerce and evolution . . .
>
> . . . The idea of evolving business strategies is appealing both as a means of generating novel ideas and as a means of optimization . . .

. . . While serious biological debate continues on the subject of punctuated or gradual mutation, we can posit that the equivalent random element for business is innovation.

And, of course, we like the model because we believe that you can't win the fight or gain control when change is happening all around you. Change occurs whether you do anything or nothing. No thing itself is immune to a changing environment and the larger dynamics of evolution. The best approach is to adapt intelligently whenever possible. Taking this view provides an interesting way to look at different kinds of innovation and how they represent different vectors of ongoing evolutionary change for business.

Within an analogy of evolution (and applying Clayton Christensen's innovation categories[8]), sustaining innovation would be similar to a set of traits emerging as an advantage to dominating opportunities. These traits, when favored above others, help continue the path of dominance. Down-market innovation would be analogous to changes in the environment that make it necessary to change habits, such as searching for different kinds of prey or moving into more friendly eco-niches. Here the traits that favored advantage are now overkill or simply add no advantage, and it's more effective to look for other opportunities, even if they don't require all of the power of the previously dominant traits. Disruptive innovation is the random genetic mutation enabling traits that happen to be favored by the current environment but that might not be successful in a different environment. These are the traits that could also prove to be the keys to survival if the environmental change is happening fast enough.

In this view, innovation is a series of ongoing processes. Like evolution, it never stops. The goal is to keep the business alive and thriving by creating value for customers across all of a business's activities, despite changes in the environment beyond its control.

Of course, the key difference between this model and natural evolution (as well as the silver bullet model) is that design does play a role! And when used intelligently, not only can it help focus invention and ideas in ways that make innovation matter (value for customers), it can also help identify and create bidirectional influences for innovation across the entire sphere of activities a business undertakes to deliver value to customers, across every touch point. We think that such a model of innovation as evolution complements our proposal for experience.

Christensen proposes that not all business can innovate successfully and that certain kinds of cultures and structures make it difficult, if not impossible, for all kinds of innovation. We can't contest this point. We do believe, however, that if innovation is relentless and driven by external change, not innovating certainly means increasing the risk of not surviving. And innovating shouldn't mean looking for silver bullets or waiting for structural change. Instead, it's about looking at opportunities for increasing value for customers across the board, not just in products and services.

If you accept that innovation is simply the means by which business, products, services, and customer experiences evolve, it follows that the important thing is having a framework to understand which areas are good candidates for adding more value and which ideas might be interesting in this light, even if they aren't the next big thing.

We had a client who reportedly asked her staff, "Why didn't we invent Pinterest?" The answer may just be that you could have, but it wouldn't have seemed big enough and therefore important enough at the time. In evolution, the random mutation is not produced through intent to ensure future survival for the species because the dominant line is threatened; it is random and luckily happens to do better with the shift in the environment. Or as Albert Einstein put it, "Innovation is not the product of logical thought, although the result is tied to logical structure."[9]

In light of this model, the idea that innovation and design should be separate and occur at different stages doesn't make sense to us. There are multiple vectors of innovation that need to be ongoing, and design (process and outcome) should be part of all the processes. Otherwise, ideas that could translate to customer value could be ignored because they don't match the problem or opportunity in the way that business is framing things (competition, efficiency, cost, revenue, etc.).

For those skeptical that design can produce innovation, we aren't making that claim. We are, however, saying that design, when used and delivered properly, with the benefit of a holistic framework for engaging customers around value, can take good ideas quite far—and can quickly show the limitations of ideas that seemed good in theory as well. After all, if the Army considers design "a methodology for applying critical and creative thinking to understand, visualize and describe complex, ill-structured problems and develop approaches to them,"[10] then we believe that business should feel comfortable using design to help turn ideas into value, too.

Add It Up: We Need Experience Design

The rate of change of information today is unprecedented. The rate of change of technology drives this and other changes for business. Products and services can literally become extinct: The economics shift dramatically and business models are no longer viable, or the value that was provided gets superseded; the context of use they once served may no longer exist.

The processes of managing a business, especially the creation of value and the role that design plays, are getting more and more complex, producing fragmented customer experiences. The results can simply be mediocre output, or they may convince customers that they have less reason to stay with a brand or business if they feel that the business doesn't value their patronage. And businesses seem to almost operate as if they expect that "once a customer, always a customer," without much effort beyond letting people know when they should be buying again.

Innovation can no longer be treated as a search for the single big game changer. Innovation isn't playing the lottery and looking for a huge one-time payoff. Innovation now needs to be an ongoing process. In *The Innovator's DNA*, Jeff Dyer, Hal Gregersen, and Clayton Christensen quote Jeff Bezos on the realities of innovating[11]:

> "You need to do as many experiments per unit of time as possible," says Bezos. "Innovation is part and parcel with going down blind alleys. You can't have one without the other. But every once in a while, you go down an alley and it opens up into this huge broad avenue . . . it makes all the blind alleys worthwhile."

If business needs to continually innovate with a focus on keeping customers engaged and providing value across the entire range of the customer life cycle (both before and after the purchase), then there needs to be a portfolio of engagement—lots of smaller bets targeted at current needs, laying the foundation for future value and exploring new opportunities based on external changes.

As Peter Sims describes it in *Little Bets*, the approach that many have taken is to look at lots of options, test them, and see which produce the best results[12]:

> At the core of this experimental approach they [innovators, creatives, entrepreneurs] use little bets to discover, test and develop ideas that are achievable and affordable. Little bets are their vehicle for discovery, whereby action produces insights that can be analyzed. . . . in order to frame, and reframe problems and ideas . . . then adapt and act using little bets.

This might suggest adopting Nassim Nicholas Taleb's advice and building in optionality. He suggests the concept of a system that benefits from volatility, not just robust, but the opposite of fragile—antifragile. According to Taleb, we do a really poor job understanding risk and tend to assume that our risk models are right when they probably aren't. His suggestion involves building in the right options for situations not fully in our control or where information is not yet conclusive. Doing this means not getting sucked into making bets with small upsides but large risks but rather making bets that have small risks with potentially higher upsides, even if the odds are long.[13] We like the idea of design helping to create antifragile products, services, and experiences for business.

We expect to see more and more businesses begin to move this way, and many are already taking many of these approaches. We believe that this can be more effective and potentially an easier transition to make if there is some heuristic or framework that allows businesses to begin change and keep the outcomes integrated.

To do this, businesses will need to become more proficient in evaluating how and where they place efforts to quickly see which ideas have the potential to add value for customers and which ones won't. With an attitude of more bets and fewer sure things, there is also an opportunity to hedge these bets by having efforts be mutually reinforcing, strengthening the customers' perception of value that they get across their entire relationship with the business.

We believe that our experience design model can help businesses make a smarter transition and gain assistance from design in more effective ways. We see it as a framework that allows businesses to leverage their brands throughout the entire customer experience, make sure that products and services deliver value, ensure that customer experiences don't become fragmented, and lead to higher engagement and higher lifetime value per customer.

4

Thinking about Experience Design

The learned man is not the man who provides the correct responses, rather he is the man who poses the right questions.

—Claude Lévi-Strauss[1]

In *The Price of Fish*, Michael Mainelli and Ian Harris caution us against seeking precision in our understanding of problems and outcomes. They state that acknowledging possible outcomes is okay, and they see it not as a lack of precision but instead as a "sign of maturity." We are fond of the quote from John von Neumann with which they drive the point home[2]:

> There's no point in being precise when you don't even know what you are talking about.

Precision has long been a core value in business and design. Certainty is a desired context for many business decisions, and often we implicitly assume that problems are clearly understood and that the outcome can be predicted to a greater or lesser degree. The application of formal systems of design often thrives on iterative cycles in which all the kinks and rough edges can get worked out.

But what if this is no longer possible? What if time to market makes quality both a benefit and a risk? What if things are changing too rapidly to establish which aspects of quality will actually make a difference in the marketplace? What happens when business puts known costs of efficiency ahead of the unknown cost of a dissatisfied customer? Is there a way to predict which trade-offs in the quality of an experience are important? How do you move forward into the unknown with at least some degree of confidence?

We want to help business and design start having conversations in which these kinds of issues can be intelligently tackled, even if neither side is an expert (there are very few experts or reliable information sources on the future, and betting on past models during periods of disruption doesn't seem to be highly rewarding). Ironically, many of the approaches that have worked in the past may not have been based on data that were more reliable or sound than of the data we have for the future. It just may be that the rate of change was slower, so our errors were not as apparent at that time.

We propose a simple scenario to illustrate how easy it is to ignore the role that information plays. If you are asked to stand in the middle of your living room at high noon and get outside within 3 seconds, it will likely prove to be a very simple task. If you try to do the exact same thing at 2 AM with no lights on, in the house or outside, it will prove much more difficult. That's because you have insufficient data to meet the speed of change that you are putting yourself into. Forget precision; you don't even know which way you are facing.

In the first case, you have as much data as you need, and the rate of data feedback based on your actions is instantaneous (essentially because the only thing moving is you). You probably aren't even thinking about the information available and how you use it. In the second case, not only do you not know exactly where you are or where you're headed, but an "update" of data might prove highly problematic—coming in the form of a banged shin as you run into a coffee table, or worse, a bruised nose as you face-plant into a wall. If business and design have been collaborating in the past in a way similar to the lit room scenario, the future is likely to be much closer to the dark room version, with the twist that once outside the front door, we may find that we're not even in Kansas anymore.

How do we know if a proposed product or service will actually be valuable to a customer? At what point is it possible for us to be sure? How do we know how much of the value that a customer experiences is a result of having a need met or a result of the way the product or service meets the need? Looking to position design as the

UNIVERSITY OF WINCHESTER
LIBRARY

ingredient that makes things more valuable assumes that the basic premise is already valuable. If the execution is not seen as valuable (or effective), then clearly it's the design that's at fault—not the basic premise. If design's ability to deliver value can be constrained when information is restricted or seen as not relevant by the business commissioning the design, imagine the outcome when the business is in the dark as well.

If we are concerned with business success and how business uses design in the most efficient way possible, then we suggest that the foundation element to focus on is the creation of value that customers will care about and will continue to engage with over time.

We believe that experience design is a strategic framework that allows a business to collaborate more effectively with design with the goal of creating value and engaging customers, even as the larger environmental context changes. We think that it provides the right structure for helping differentiate your company from competitors as well as approaching innovation and reacting to external change in a more informed and antifragile manner.

As we said in the Introduction, we are putting this forth with the hope of starting a larger conversation about this approach. Although we will follow with more tactical frameworks and tools for beginning to put the thinking in action, we aren't putting forth a precise model or recipe for success. If we could do that, this would be a much more expensive book.

Considering Experience

Think of the experiences you've had in your life that have had the most impact on who you are today—what kind of person you are, your values, how you view success, and how you believe others should be treated. If you are like many people, you will have several significant experiences that you can point to: a person—perhaps a relative, a teacher, a mentor—who helped you to understand an aspect of the world; events—things you saw, took part in, and heard about; and situations—circumstances involving you and other people, events, resources, opportunities, constraints—that forced you to make and accept certain decisions and see what happened as a result. As you think about these significant experiences, you may notice some interesting things happening. Your memory may run a bit free, as you recall what actually happened and begin to remember details and tangents from different periods of your life. You may feel waves of emotion pass through you as the memories trigger certain ideas and feelings.

What you are doing is focusing on a basic process, an action that is a fundamental part of the human existence: the use of information that you have received through various means to form an opinion about what the world outside of you is about and how things there are likely to work. Each experience is the set of information you have noticed and stored, along with your emotional and rational responses that arose from the process of receiving the information and making sense of it at the moment of occurrence, modified through the reinforcement or weakening of these perceptions based on other experiences that have accumulated over time.

The emerging understanding of human consciousness currently points to some similarities between the human mind and a computer. Some might even go so far as to draw a complete connection, saying that our minds are essentially computers that look at the probabilities of outcomes based on the information received. In this way, our mind is continuously building a statistical model of how the external world is likely to behave and our likely reaction to it. From how we acquire language as infants and how it shapes our thinking to the scientific method that has been a driving force behind the expansion of technology that now continues to redefine what is possible, this model of the brain as experience builder and possibility statistician is compelling. Perhaps the most interesting aspect is that much of this occurs in ways that are largely outside of our conscious focus. We aren't always aware that we are learning, but what we learn affects our thinking.

Now think about the experiences you have when buying and using products and services. Many of the components of these experiences happen without much thought. It's only when things depart from the expected that we take note. One of our favorite examples here is what we call the "Oh . . . shit!" moment. This can happen when buying something that you are not overly familiar with but that you will use to enable some other activity or interest that is very important to you. The name arises from what you say when you get home, open the package, and realize that you either (1) got the wrong thing, (2) got the right thing but it's incompatible with what you hoped to use it with, or (3) still need an additional component to actually use what you just got.

Or consider the last time that you spoke with tech support or customer service about an issue you were having with a product or a service. Have you ever ended up not only learning that your problem was not a problem but also discovering more value in the product or service than you were expecting? The common experience is that there is a problem and, often, one without a quick solution.

Last, consider a product or service you have been using for the past few years. What is the difference between your feelings as you use it now versus your feelings during the first few encounters after you made the purchase? These last three examples have an implicit component that we didn't mention, but it's part of the process involved in buying a product or service. At some point in time, you built an expectation in your mind, based on some level of information provided to you and your understanding of what your needs were and how you intended to fulfill them. As the examples illustrate, in many situations, there can be a big gap between what you expected and what actually occurred. If you're straightforward with yourself, it's likely that you'll accept some degree of responsibility for this gap (especially if your enthusiasm to acquire something got the better of your common sense to make sure you knew what you were getting into). But there are probably cases you remember in which you did your homework and still wound up with a gap, and the result was an unfavorable view of the business you dealt with, even if the company was not intentionally trying to deceive you or misrepresent its offer. Think about how likely you would be to engage with the business again.

The point of these examples is that you are either operating without much awareness of the business behind the product or service because things are going well, or you are extremely aware of the business because things are not going well at all. Experiences that lead to higher engagement are generally good for business. Experiences that don't lead to higher levels of engagement are generally bad for business. One of the main problems is that this quality of experience (or lack thereof) is often a result of very primary decisions made about products, services, and communications during their planning and development. Often, design is asked to alleviate issues or create an acceptable presentation, but its impact is very shallow, sometimes only skin-deep. Sometimes this is because no one understands the implications of the decisions being made. Other times it's because some aspects of the experience are considered inconsequential and not worth the cost to address. When trying to implement business objectives in a timely and cost-efficient way, it's easy to forget how people actually behave and make assumptions about what people will do or how they will think, because given the information that we are looking at, our assumptions are logical and feel safe. This lack of consideration for how people will react can be a problem for business.

If you were to do an audit of current published work about people, their behavior, and their cognitive processes, you might decide to reframe your perspective quite a bit and think more about how people might react. What we have seen suggests that:

- People are a lot less rational than they think they are.

- Perception is often strongly affected by the situation or context, or how something is presented.

- People can focus very intently but at the expense of really seeing what is outside of our focus, often ignoring things that are obvious and important to consider. Whether we're looking for something we've misplaced or we're preoccupied about something else, we may miss things that are in plain sight; they simply don't register.

- People are prone to being guided by their inner belief systems without consciously understanding that it's happening.

- We tend to look for confirmation of things we already agree with and tend to ignore things that don't match our beliefs.

- People have difficulty understanding trade-offs involving benefits and long periods of time, often taking less now rather than more later. It's harder for us to resist the temptation to get the quick reward.

- Human memory is not an accurate recording of the events in which we took part or observed. We may believe that we saw or did something, it may feel real, but it also may have never happened or at least may have happened in a very different way.

- There's a difference between how we feel when we experience things and how we remember them. We tend to evaluate based on what happened during the latter parts of an experience and remember the most intense levels of the experience—we can have a reasonably good time, but if it ended abruptly or badly, that's all we take away.

- People like others to accept blame. When people have suffered what they consider to be an injustice or unfair treatment by a business, they're willing to forgive the business if the business accepts blame rapidly, even if the business can't fix the problem right away.

In the book *Thinking, Fast and Slow*, author Daniel Kahneman, a Nobel Prize winner in Economic Sciences, describes the differences between how we perceive the world, how we act based on our perceptions, and what actually tends to happen.[3]

One of the points we take away from this is that if people don't act in a rational way, then making decisions that favor economy of effort based on the expectation that people will be rational is not going to work out very well. It also suggests that people won't necessarily understand trade-offs that they enter into, even if it seems pretty clear to one side of an interaction that a trade-off is being made. No one expects an economy brand to provide a luxury service, but it's not uncommon to see people complaining about the level of service they get from an economy brand. Is this the fault of the buyer or the seller? We suggest that it's both. Not anticipating this kind of irrationality is what sets the situation up in the first place.

But why should obvious misinterpretations come back to haunt us? Once the logic of the situation is revealed, can't we expect people to behave with a bit more rationality and accept their role in the problem? Not necessarily, especially since we're often unaware of what is really triggering our emotions and driving our responses.

Dr. David Rock is in the business of coaching executives and is also the founder and chief executive officer of the NeuroLeadership Group, a global consulting and training firm. He combined his experiences in coaching managers with his research in neuroscience in a book called *Your Brain at Work*. It describes what's actually going on as we experience work, both managing and being managed. One of the foundational premises of the book is that what's going on in the brain at a chemical level affects how we experience and react to the world. Although this is very enlightening for managers, it's also useful for understanding experiences, especially how customers experience interactions with products and services and the businesses that provide them.

To summarize, Dr. Rock describes the brain as consisting of systems, some operating at a conscious level and some at a subconscious level. Sensory input triggers activity in the systems, and this can produce chemicals, which either make us feel good or make us feel stressed. He describes five systems that are important in everyday human experiences using the acronym SCARF as a mnemonic: status, certainty, autonomy, relatedness, and fairness. What we consciously experience is affected by how these systems are being activated and what the resulting chemical response is based on the input.[4]

He points out that two of these systems have very strong influences on us, almost as powerful as the systems that drive us toward food and sex. These two systems are status and fairness. Humans tend to not take slights to status or perceptions of inequity lying down. In fact, Dr. Rock describes individuals whose lives have been drastically affected by issues that negatively impact their sense of status or fairness. The converse is true as well, and we can feel very good when these are triggered to produce positive impacts.

Think about the old maxims "The customer is king" and "The customer is always right," and they take on an entirely different meaning. We also now understand better why small slights that shouldn't logically be an issue can be, and why thinking about how experiences engage customers becomes extremely relevant all the time. It also would follow as relatively obvious that a thin layer of good design isn't going to turn a poor attempt to deliver value into a good experience.

In the real world, people tend to get beyond surface appearances pretty quickly—it's only a matter of time. When we interact directly with products and services, we begin to understand how inaccurate our initial impressions may have been. We often find that what things look like is not directly connected to the way things work—or don't work. In many cases, we also find that there are things that happen that we didn't anticipate, or even that the relationship between how different parts work seems nonobvious, perhaps even random. If the approach to designing products, services, and experiences isn't done correctly, the perception of value can erode quite rapidly. And if expectations were already set too high, even an adequate experience can seem less than adequate.

When people use a product or a service, they are interacting with all the positives and negatives, even if the latter are mere oversights. But they may quickly lead to negative interpretations of the experience and get attributed to the business that provides them. In many cases the business has invested in and used brand as a means to communicate with customers. The positive or negative experiences can lead to an interpretation of the validity and integrity of the brand.

The role of experience is not just about understanding how people respond to intentional value but also about understanding how people respond to problems and issues that may have never been considered. But it can easily get worse. As we pointed out in earlier chapters, the focus of design by business is often on the presales side of the customer experience, and what happens to a customer post-sales might not get the level of attention it deserves. Many companies ask too much of their customers and make them bounce between call centers, online forms, and FAQs. Customers see and hear different things at different times, lose track of what they're supposed to do, and get stuck at different critical moments. Employees, even when well trained and enthusiastic, are at a big disadvantage when faced with a customer who is already confused, frustrated, and in the midst of a bad experience.

In a 2010 Forrester study, 90 percent of companies with annual revenues of $500 million or more thought it was either "critical" or "very important" that customer experience was in a company's strategy. And 80 percent wanted to be able to differentiate their company with customer experience.[5]

Remarkably, only 15 percent of respondents said that their companies do "very well" in maintaining a consistent user experience across all communications channels. And the challenges are growing as organizations address sales, service, and support options via a growing tangle of channels, including contact centers, websites, branch offices, agents in the field, mail and fax, e-mail, and mobile tools and apps. It's easy to see how improved levels of service for all areas of the customer experience can help build stronger relationships, and we agree. Customer service is not necessarily concerned with how a product, service, or solution is defined, designed, or delivered, though, nor is it necessarily concerned with how the use derives value through use. Customer service is often problem-focused, whereas we believe that businesses need to be value-focused and leverage the intent and meaning of the brand into value, not just problem solving.

It's clear that business is not setting out to create poor experiences. They often hire what they believe to be the best design resources to get it right. The problem is that there often is no strategy for making sure that business and design make the right choices. Without this there is no ability to broaden the influence design has and prevent it from being a Band-Aid applied as the last stage before a mediocre experience provokes a less than rational response.

We acknowledge that the business operations, the development and delivery of value, and the servicing of customers and business partners is a highly complex system, and we don't suggest that there are quick fixes to making everything produce top-level value all the time. But there needs to be a way for business to get more out of the efforts they make, and we believe that shifting the thinking to an experience-centric approach can help make changes over time that add up.

Setting the Strategic Stage for Experience Design

Systems thinking essentially looks at all the components of a system in order to better understand all of the requirements, parameters, interdependencies, and true impact of decisions. It is especially appropriate when working on very complex problems, often called wicked problems. (*The Price of Fish* and *The Wide Lens* are both examples of systems thinking approaches.) We like systems thinking, but believe it misses a key point when applied to business and design: Why would one business take a certain approach, and why would a competitor do something different? In one sense, systems thinking is a heuristic for developing strategy but not a strategy by itself. Youngme Moon illustrates in *Different* that businesses can take different approaches based on how they choose to use their brand, their relationship to customers, and the market opportunity. This is why we think systems thinking needs more grounding. We have also seen processes such as design thinking and user-centered design being used as a more effective approach to creating value for customers. We think these are effective approaches, but they are tactics that should be used during problem solving.

We have worked with strategists who suggest that business strategy comes first and foremost and say all else serves business strategy. We argue that if that strategy is not based on value and customers, it is on shaky ground. We also argue that if you concede that value and customers are core components of strategy, then Brand (with a capital B—the big idea, not just the name or the logo) is the best summation we currently have on hand for the ways in which business, value, and customers tend to organize and behave. We raise this point because it will be necessary to consider Brand from a strategic point of view as we illustrate how experience design can become a framework for collaboration between business and design.

But first we should deal with some other baggage that can accompany using Brand this way. The first is the assertion that since Brands are built over time, thinking of Brand as a core component is irrelevant in many cases, especially if a business is a start-up or if the market in which a business operates doesn't typically compete on Brand. We believe that any business that has customers and does business under a fixed name has a Brand, whether they want to acknowledge this or not. In this case, the Brand is the set of elements used to distinguish the relationship between the business and its customers. It may be one-dimensional or it may be multidimensional, but it is clear that there is some kind of relationship based on the exchange of value (products, services, or solutions for money). Once the process starts, the Brand begins to accrue meaning, either intentionally or unintentionally. It may have very little impact or leverage, but all the experiences that occur during the exchange of value are being associated with the business and therefore whatever Brand the business has established.

A second assertion that comes up is that Brands are something intangible, without real value, and somehow are only really manifested through branding, which generally falls under the marketing function in most modern businesses. As such, it's not a primary component of strategy. Branding as defined by applying the logo to products, services, and solutions through advertising, communications, packaging, collateral, signage, and so on, is a component of Brand management. Although important, it is often influenced by the goals of strategy. But branding is not Brand. Brand becomes a promise of what the company stands for and offers to the customer. In this way, branding elevates ideas from being visual identifiers of who is providing value to expectations about the value itself. Once you set expectations around value for customers, you quickly begin to influence the ability to deliver on strategic goals and objectives (or not). In this sense, Brand is simply another way of representing strategy, and if the way it is represented is wrong or the decisions about enacting strategy and the expectations you're creating for the customer don't match up, the strategy may become compromised.

A third assertion that has been gaining traction over the past decade is that companies no longer own their Brand and that it is now owned by the customers. This is partly true. Gone are the days when consistent, unilateral communication about what a Brand stands for will convince people to buy the products and services of that Brand. The evaluation of value is increasingly based on experience—did my experience as a buyer match up with the expectation that the Brand set? In addition, with the efficiencies of communication technology, the message about expectation gaps from real people and real customers is often reaching consumers with as much influence as the message put out by the Brand, if not more. But customers do not invest, prior to buying, in what a business is going to create as value. They do not go to the business and tell them what to make, how to deliver it, and share in the risk if the decision is wrong. Customers also do not tell businesses how ideas and concepts that a Brand may rest on should be converted to actual, buyable value. (We understand that many businesses do have strong relationships with customers that

—

Figure 4.1
Brand as Arising from All of a Business's Activities

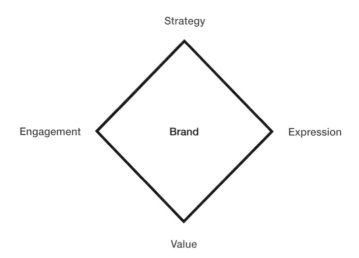

affect product and service strategies, but a large percentage of these are likely to be based on existing products and services and how the business can make them better, not on what a business should invest in doing and why.)

Businesses own their Brands inasmuch as they are responsible for managing them and making decisions about how they are used. Customers react, and it is true to say that customers now define Brand meaning for themselves (based on experience), but this does not mean customers own the Brand.

To raise Brand to the strategic level, we use the diagram shown in Figure 4.1 working with our clients. We represent Brand as a diamond and propose it as a representation of the business through four connected areas: strategy, expression, value, and engagement:

> Strategy: The corporate strategy (including mission, vision, and core meaning for the Brand and positioning) and the functional components of strategy that affect explicit areas of the business (such as technology strategy, product/service strategy, and market strategy)

> Expression: The articulation of identity—how the company is recognized and distinguished from others in communications (advertising, marketing) and all aspects of presenting the company (graphic systems and applications such as trade dress)

> Value: The actual products, services, and solutions a company might put into the market; includes the tangible, intangible, and aspirational value they provide

> Engagement: How people outside the company (press, partners, and most important, customers) interact with and interpret what the business is doing (the manifestation of strategy, expression, and value). This includes the basic journey from awareness to consideration, purchase, and use of the brand, as well as the cycles of the customer relationship with the business over time. Experiences are delivered through a range of touch points and mechanisms, some owned and controlled by the Brand and some outside of it.

If you draw a circle around the diamond, as shown in Figure 4.2, you now have defined the entire set of components of the experience that is created through the reality of that business operating and serving customers.

Experience design takes the view that the nature of the actual value provided to customers, along with the nature of the experiences customers have over time and across touch points, will define how customers feel about the business, how they interpret its Brand, and how they reflect the true nature of the business.

Experience design focuses on managing this system over time with the goal of keeping customers engaged around value for as long as possible. It should also be understood that the environment this circle sits in is ever changing (in ways beyond anyone's direct control).

Experience design is not the same as customer service design, nor is it organization or business process design. It's the design for all of the activities that most effectively bring the brand to life through real value for the customer and the development of a

Figure 4.2

Experience Design Addresses the Totality of All the Elements of the Business, Brand, and Customer

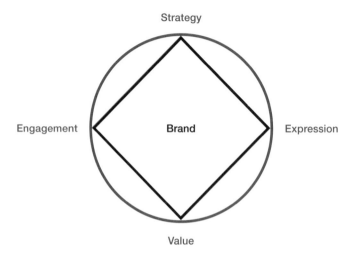

level of intent and quality in everything done on behalf of the customer. Again, the emphasis is on the *why,* not just the *how.*

It's tempting to take a more pragmatic view of the world and simply connect strategy and value, as illustrated in Figure 4.3, leaving expression and engagement for marketing and design to manage. This is what we believe a lot of business leaders have a tendency to do. It's interesting to see the outcome of this approach. Two triangles form by bisecting the diamond from strategy to value. The triangle on the right portion of this diagram is the business's point of view (POV) and represents the intent of the business. The triangle on the left portion is the customer's POV and represents how they see things. There is an inherent problem that happens when splitting the model this way, as it allows a kind of false logic to set in: It makes sense from an internal perspective; therefore, it will make sense to an external view.

One of our business's first and longest client relationships was with Autodesk, a global provider of design software for creating virtually any aspect of the human-made world. Most of our work was done with Shane Brentham, who managed the worldwide marketing organization at Autodesk for a number of years. He used to caution against the tendency for enterprises to allow their organizational structure to dictate how the customer experiences the Brand. His point was that it's easy for a business unit to make decisions that are advantageous for themselves but that may not be in the best interest of the Brand or the customer in the long run. As we stated before, as long as a business operates, whatever happens between it and its customers is attributed to whatever form of representation it uses (expression), and

Figure 4.3
Dividing the Brand into Two Halves: The Business View and the Customer View

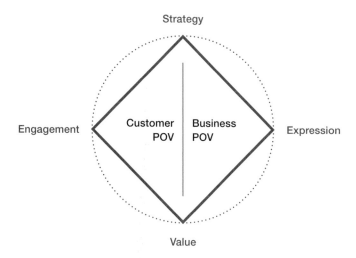

there are experiences and outcomes that customers will have (engagement). Stated another way, everything rolls uphill and accretes to the Brand, whether you plan it that way or not.

We believe that making decisions with an eye focused only on the right side of the circle is a mistake, yet we continually see businesses taking this approach. When the customer perspective is taken, it's often an incomplete picture, focused on what's next for value or problem alleviation through support. Instead they should be asking, Is the overall experience still engaging the customer in a way that delivers value?

Principles of Experience Design

In his book *Frames of Mind*, Howard Gardner describes how the progress made by Western science in the past was largely attributable to the development of differential and integral calculus[6]:

> Chemistry and physics are concerned with explaining change—the evolution of physical systems—not the description of steady states. Without the calculus, the process of dealing with such changes would be very difficult. But with calculus, it's possible to determine how the change of one quantity relates to the other quantities connected to it.

If design has become a tool that business uses to focus on specific points or states in the creation and delivery of value, the complexity of all the components of the experience that business needs to manage and the rate and fluidity of "environmental" change would suggest the need for new tools. Although it is in no way a science or even a predictive tool, we like the analogy of experience design as the calculus for businesses to use in building engagement around value for their brand and customers.

The primary building blocks of experience design are:

Time	Brand Intent
The recognition that change is constant. This perspective allows the scope of context for any problem, product, service, or experience to be expanded in ways that uncover useful information, opportunities, and interdependencies.	Who you are as a business and what you stand for. This provides a guide for the kind of value the business is producing and the attributes and qualities (not just the look) that should differentiate the experience of doing business with the company; this is not the same thing as branding.
Products, Services, and Solutions	Engagement Experience
The actual value customers are paying for in the first place. These must deliver on clear value propositions in a consistent manner over time and meet reasonable customer expectations.	Where, when, and how you interact with customers. This defines how business engages and manages the customer relationship over time (not just when the business is in sales mode).

Using experience design as an approach is based on frameworks and tools that help both business and design tackle problems with an objective view as to basic criteria upon which a solution should deliver.

These rely on the following principles:

---

1   There is a real cost for value. Qualities and attributes that cannot be tied to value for the customer are a luxury and should be applied only after a basic level of value exists.

....

2   The benefits and outcomes produced by design become compromised when design is treated as a stage-gate for completing a solution that has already been "approved" by a business-only evaluation process.

....

3   There will be more ability to engage customers when the Brand, the products and services it delivers, and the experiences customers have remain aligned over time and are focused on the business delivering value to the customer.

....

4   There is no such thing as "Build it and they will come."
Engagement is always based on:

$$\text{Perceived Value} \quad > \quad \text{Cognitive Overhead}$$

....

5   Just because you captured a customer's attention or money doesn't mean that person is satisfied and will stay a customer. A person will remain a customer only as long as they perceive value:

$$\text{Perceived Value} = \frac{\left(\begin{array}{c} \text{What has been done or} \\ \text{provided by a business} \end{array} \right) - \left[\left(\begin{array}{c} \text{Customer} \\ \text{needs} \end{array} \right) \times \left(\begin{array}{c} \text{Customer} \\ \text{expectations} \end{array} \right) \right]}{\text{Customer context}}$$

....

6   An engaged customer is of more value to a business than a nonengaged customer (especially in the service business).

....

7   Understanding and targeting emerging needs of existing customers is a base level of innovation that should be a standard operating procedure.

....

8   When products and services are enabled by technology, they become more effective at providing full solutions, but by definition, this shifts expectations to what happens on an ongoing basis, rather than at a single point in time.

....

9   The pace of technology change means that relentless innovation is the norm and is not restricted to specific industries and sectors.

....

10   With customers evaluating relationships over many interactions over time, there are a lot more places where a business/brand can make mistakes; management is a job that never ends.

The purpose of these elements and principles of experience design as a concept and a process is to help translate the Brand into engaging value and to reinforce Brand meaning through the real experiences of real people.

Figure 4.4 shows how these two flows of meaning operate. Realizing that time plays an important part in the concept of experience design is important for understanding the concept as well as using it at a tactical and implementation level.

The downstream flow from the business begins with the definition of Brand. When done correctly, Brand is a guide for the value propositions of the products and services offered by the business. If everything goes well, customers perceive the value as the business intended.

The upstream flow from customers begins with the experiences they have around value with products and services, from initial awareness through to purchase and use. If there is real value and the perception of value can be strengthened through the experience of how the business conducts the relationship after the initial purchase

—

Figure 4.4

How Intention and Experience Lead to a Brand's Meaning and a Customer's Belief in That Meaning

Business

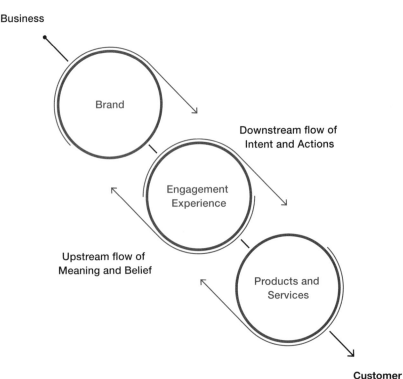

(which includes support but also how the business continues to communicate and engage the customer on an ongoing basis), this contributes to the closing of the cycle as customers give meaning to the Brand.

We also want to point out that design is best considered as both the process and the outcome; experience design acknowledges that for business, the need to optimize experiences around value, especially through change, is not a one-time, or piecemeal, process. It's ongoing. And it's about creating a framework through which business and design can collaboratively apply systems thinking to the problem of creating value and engaging customers.

There are many touch points to consider and an increasing need to enable customers to move seamlessly across and between them. Translating knowledge, intent, and insights into a customer experience for every touch point has become a complex task. This complexity is unlikely to slow. People rarely experience a brand in isolation; they experience a brand over the course of time in many different situations and derive value and meaning from the totality. Every touch point should be viewed as an opportunity to drive further levels of engagement with customers. The better the experience, the more loyalty gained. Design plays a critical role.

Experience design is based on the belief that business can be intentional and opportunistic (in a good way) by managing the business and the Brand to create competitive advantage by building value-based relationships that are difficult for a competitor to fully reproduce, and function in the classic sense of Brand in which there is equity through loyalty, recommendation, and price elasticity. This allows for a smarter and more informed approach to innovation by making ongoing small bets that create value and minimize risk, even as the surrounding environment rapidly shifts.

In his seminal work on design theory and patterns in architecture, Christopher Alexander speaks about the relationship between a pattern or solution and the context to which it applies. The basic premise is that if the context doesn't accurately represent the need, the pattern or solution that has been defined to solve the problem will be ineffective. In this case, we suggest thinking about context as the circle around the information that is deemed as important and relevant. If the circle excludes key information, there's a problem. If the circle includes too much information, there can be issues as well, as the problem becomes too complex to solve (as Shane Brentham used to say, you can't boil the ocean).

In 2011, Marc Shillum joined Method as a principal guiding our Brand practice. He was very interested in extending his thinking of Brands as patterns into our thinking around experience design. Shillum's point of view was that people have a proclivity to see patterns as a way of making sense of the world, and as such, Brands should be considering how their actions are guided by intentional patterns of artifacts (objects), behaviors (experiences), and concepts (meaning) in order to produce coherent experiences over time that become recognizable by customers. Shillum had intuitively come to the same conclusion that we had reached about the upstream influence on brand that experience had, and it was not a huge leap of logic to see how a more intentional and systematic view would allow the business to better use the Brand in the downstream flow. Our belief is that this downstream flow is also where experience design and innovation intersect.

What separates experience design from pure systems thinking is this focus on Brand and how it can serve as the DNA for all of the activities involved in creating value and engaging customers. But for the experience design approach to tap into this, the Brand has to be seen as a central element of business that is codeveloped and managed by the business-minded and the design-minded. Even when there's a dearth of available information, business and design still have a framework for building suppositions and extrapolations and producing a solution that can be highly successful.

One of the goals of experience design is to make sure that the right breadth of information is considered, even if it's not absolute or statistically validated. This is where the role of time comes in. Time can be used to explore different scenarios and ask questions that can point to information (or the lack thereof) that can be beneficial to creating more value.

Following are the basic ways in which time should be considered:

- What potential situations will customers be in, and what would be of most value to them while still aligning with the business goals?

- What most likely preceded the current customer situation, and what are the next steps, driven by customer need, to help further engagement between customers and the business?

- What other parallel processes or touch points are relevant to consider (including other businesses, products, services, and solutions)?

- What are areas of change outside of the current focus that might influence perceptions of value in the near future?

In some ways the problem is very similar to playing a game of chess. One has to consider the current situation but think through many "what if" scenarios and successive stages of play before committing to an actual move. In some cases the move may be quite small in immediate impact but set up for a more powerful finish. One can see this only after expanding the perspective and analysis forward through time and accounting for many possible variations of response.

Figure 4.5 illustrates how any project that is intended to create value for a customer would be approached through experience design. The basic premise is to make sure that within the context of the project, the following three considerations are considered and resolved in a way that matches business and customer goals using design (in the full sense of the term) for both processes and outputs.

Consideration 1: Solve for *why*. Any project should begin with a clear statement of why the business is doing what it's doing and why this is valuable for the customer. There may be many degrees of separation between the two, but ostensibly there will always be some connection. If we can't posit that there is value, it raises two questions: (1) Are we considering a broad enough circle of information to understand why it is valuable? and (2) If we're sure we have considered every angle and we still can't determine any value, why is it being done?

Identifying, articulating, and prioritizing requirements is an effective way to look at what a solution needs to deliver and to be clear enough about the intention of the requirements to be sure that they are likely to provide value to the customer. In many cases, business leaders may have a general idea about what they want a product to do but are unable to articulate the requirements that would deliver upon the goal. There can be effective cost savings for businesses as well if they can weed out unnecessary ideas that have no real business case or customer value.

Figure 4.5
Relationship of Universal Inputs and Project-Specific Inputs
Under an Experience Design Approach

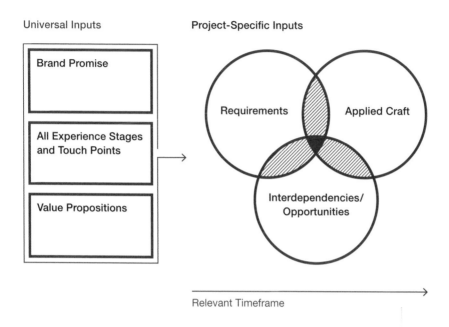

Universal Inputs   Project-Specific Inputs

Brand Promise

All Experience Stages
and Touch Points

Value Propositions

Requirements   Applied Craft

Interdependencies/
Opportunities

Relevant Timeframe

Consideration 2: Make sure the how reflects the character of the Brand and enhances value. The focus should be on identifying how the value for the customer can be enhanced (through the craft of design) in a way that differentiates the Brand and supports business goals. The point we want to stress here is that coming up with a great how doesn't mean much if the why was never answered. And sometimes less is more—a compelling answer to why is better than an exceptional execution of how.

One of the purposes of this step is to make sure that the approach taken to delivering value isn't hijacked by a particular design discipline. Visual design, interaction design, interface design, industrial design, environmental design, technology design—every one of these has a high level of craft that can be applied to a given problem. But it's rare that a single discipline can provide all the answers.

It's becoming increasingly common to hear a designer describe himself or herself as an experience designer or to hear references that all design is experience design. This is great. We encourage designers to think more about designing for experience; however, we also believe that there is a dangerous tautological belief that can follow, that is, the belief that a designer's choice and recommended solution will produce a better experience than one suggested by a nondesigner. The challenge is that the experience of design in the real world is multifaceted. As such, only a multifaceted approach to problem solving can begin to address the myriad requirements and possibilities.

It may seem odd that we're explaining principles of experience design yet we're brushing aside the importance of how the design (as output) behaves. There is also the question, why isn't all design experience design? There is great temptation to look at techniques used for how value is delivered and equate them with value. In 1999 a seminal book on service thinking was introduced, and it had the arresting title: *The Experience Economy: Work Is Theater & Every Business a Stage.* Authors B. Joseph Pine II and James H. Gilmore detailed how the shift from products to services in our economy raised the importance on the *how* of experience and that in many cases this how was both the core value that the customer was paying for and the competitive advantage certain businesses had over others.[7] We agree that an experience can be delightful. But delight should be considered in a subjective sense. What delights you when you have a flat tire in the middle of nowhere is likely to be a tow truck; during a delay in business travel, it may be an upgrade to business class; and during a stressful day, maybe a message from a loved one that simply expresses happiness that you are there for him or her.

There is no question that behavior, aesthetics, materials, human response, and craftsmanship are all important. They are, after all, the components from which experiences are made. But we think that our approach to experience keeps the discussion of these aspects of design at the implementation level—the how of delivering value, not the why.

It's too easy to get seduced into believing that customers will agree that the experience is valuable when there may not be enough value to keep customers engaged. The craft of design can have an immense impact, but we think it can only enhance core value, not replace it.

We also believe that the pace of technology change means that there will always be an opportunity for a business or its competitors to produce a novelty and to create an experience that others don't have. However, in most cases, these will not be timeless. Others will quickly follow suit, or the novelty will wear off and the question will come back to: Does the customer get enough value to continue to want to pay? This is especially true for services and solutions. We believe that framing experience design the way we have helps businesses more effectively differentiate products and services, deliver a higher level of value, and create lasting relationships.

The other crucial part of this step is being able to translate the Brand into meaningful inputs that actually describe or inform the question of how. This can be a big challenge because a Brand often starts in the boardroom as a presentation deck, and the assets available to downstream teams tend to be logos and guidelines. Developing an actionable understanding of Brand in terms of behaviors and experiential qualities that can be used to inform the development of and serve as evaluation criteria for the solutions of how is the best way to differentiate a Brand.

Consideration 3: Identify all of the key interdependencies and opportunities. What information might be missing, and what's the best way to deal with it? To some degree, this begins with asking why and seeking to understand where the Brand can influence the how, but there are several other ways that we suggest this be done. The first is to use a customer journey framework. This allows teams to expand their view and understand what the likely states of mind and need are for a customer before, during, and after using a product or service. It also helps team members begin to think about what the rest of the business might be doing that might affect or be affected by the problem they're trying to solve.

The second is to expand beyond the current set of requirements that are being solved for to try to understand what would be a logical progression of value. This may be a free-form exploration, or it may be tightly bound to a product or service road map. In either case there are benefits and opportunities. One of these is a realization that in order to support future needs, certain requirements need to be added or supported in ways that weren't being considered. Another is the realization that there may be things of significantly higher value that could easily be included with the scope of effort and would increase value for customers at no real additional expense. A final one could be that a completely different idea can emerge through the process—a true innovation that no one could have predicted but that clearly has high value. It may not replace the current requirements—it may even be a completely new line of business—but these kinds of innovation can occur through this process and it is not a large investment to allow this kind of investigation. In some cases it almost comes along free for the ride.

What we see as a key advantage to this approach is that the ratio of effort and expense for each of these steps—why (requirements), how (craft), and time (interdependencies and opportunities)—can be different depending on what the business is trying to accomplish. We even suggest that design be brought to the conversation before the actual project or program starts to help discuss the nature of the problem, what might come from each area of effort, what kinds of processes and time might be involved, and what kinds of skills would be needed. We believe that this approach would do much to increase the experience and value that customers see and is a far better approach for increasing the return on investment than a procurement-generated request for a proposal (RFP) will ever be.

Experience Design versus Agile

Some readers may be asking the question, How is this different from agile, lean, MVP (minimum viable product), or iterative design methodologies? We see these methodologies as complementary, functioning at a tactical level within an experience design approach. Agile is a methodology for approaching complex problems involved with developing digital products and services. Some practitioners will tell you is that agile is just waterfall development broken down into more manageable chunks. In any case, agile is going to be successful only when value for the customer is driving decisions and prioritization of efforts. Otherwise, agile is just a way to shift risk to the buyer of development services. Lean and MVP, in our opinion, are process optimization approaches based on limiting efforts to what is known and needed. A challenge for lean is ensuring that all the needed craft experience and thinking are available to the effort. As long as team members are truly multidisciplinary and objective, the right leverage from craft should be available. But it's often hard to really know if all team members will treat the importance of different areas of craft with equal importance and diligence.

The two areas that none of these methodologies guarantee in and of themselves is the ability to use Brand as a meaningful influence and differentiator and the ability to look at all aspects of the customer and business interface around value over the course of the relationship. We suggest that using these methodologies in conjunction with experience design would be more successful. We also caution against thinking that you are taking an experience design–centric approach simply because you used an agile or lean methodology.

Some readers may also be wondering about experience design's relationship to innovation, especially since we brought it up in this chapter in regard to the relationships between requirements, craft, and interdependencies/opportunities. We think that innovation would benefit from experience design as a foundation that helps innovation thrive. Consider the analogy we made in Chapter 3 between evolution, the current pressures on business, and what innovation can do to help react to environmental changes.

In *The Innovator's DNA*, Jeff Dyer, Hal Gregersen, and Clayton Christensen describe innovation as a set of behaviors: questioning, observing, networking, and experimenting.[8] We think that the nature of experience design and its emphasis on expanding information inputs, looking at interdependencies, considering time, and focusing on value for customers, is the perfect context within which ongoing innovation occurs. We see standard design techniques such as design thinking, iterative design, and user-centered design combined with processes such as agile and lean/MVP to support the behaviors of innovation. More important, we see a connection between a better understanding of requirements and the ability to deliver down-market innovations and sustaining or incremental innovation through exploration of the relationships between requirements, craft, and opportunities. We also believe that allowing for a dynamic change in focus across these three related areas, in the context of how a Brand can create value for customers, is the natural place for disruptive innovations to emerge (and form a foundation on which to encourage the development of innovation). Although we have never thought that design and innovation are the same thing, we do see them as closely related. We believe that experience design can be a framework that allows design and innovation to function together, making it easier for business to respond to change.

The fundamental problems facing business—and therefore design—are changing and will continue to do so. Formal systems of design established at one point in time will not anticipate future needs. The relationships and interdependencies between different touch points along the continuum that is the interface between a business and its customers will shift. What we need is a new approach for problem solving, one that places an emphasis on keeping customers engaged through value and that allows for coherency in the face of change. This approach would allow brands to use the meaning of the brand as a way of differentiating the experience and meeting future needs and expectations of customers.

Experience design, as we propose it, is about solving the problems of creating and identifying value for customers and creating a coherent experience across the entire interface between the business and its customers.

In Search of the Ultimate Example of Experience Design

In talking about our view of experience design with others, we usually get nods of encouragement and understanding and often additional points that help us deepen our thinking. One question we keep asking ourselves is, Why aren't more businesses adopting this view? After all, it seems self-evident, and it is not exactly rocket science. Shane Brentham (our longtime client, mentioned earlier in this chapter) provided an interesting two-part answer that probably has a lot of truth in it. The first part is timing—the people who lead businesses often entertain this kind of thinking only when they aren't under pressure to deliver financial results. When they are under pressure, this view of the world is not connected directly enough to near-term financial change to be relevant for them. The second is the need for evidence—he believes that most businesses would generally agree with the premise but rarely make the effort to change without seeing evidence that it has been done successfully by other similar businesses.

Ironically, the company we see as the poster child for experience design—Apple— is often seen as being successful because of its superficial design, from the iMac to the iPad era. And the follow-up is usually that the only reason that Apple could do this was because Steve Jobs controlled design.

A few weeks after Steve Jobs died, we wrote a blog post about what Jobs had helped Apple accomplish. Our view was that from the beginning, Apple had taken the value of computing—the promise of digital technology—and made it accessible to a broad audience. It did this by understanding that if the power of computing could be made into an easily usable tool that didn't require a lot of training and support, more people would be able to use it.

Our main "interfaces" with the world, as humans, are the five senses, the use of language (written and oral), and our hands. Apple products have always done a great job of reducing complexity to the point where most people can have the power of computing at their fingertips, literally and figuratively. And Apple understood that the value of a single product could be extended into an ecosystem of products and services. In this way, not only did it deliver a full solution, but it often redefined the original needs and use cases for which the products were intended.

But Apple didn't rest at simply bringing all this power to a user's fingertips through hardware and software designs that accentuated the user's control. It realized that this control needed to extend beyond the products and services and into the purchase and out-of-box experiences. This is an example of a company that has truly used the *why* and the *how* to shape the possibilities for experiencing value that define a Brand. The result has been that Apple customers tend to be highly engaged with the products, services, and the brand.

It will be up to future assessment and evaluation to determine whether Apple's success was the result of a single-minded visionary or whether it can continue to function through the application of an approach like experience design. But we think it's incorrect to attribute Apple's success solely to the outcome of design or the control of a single person.

We believe that using an approach such as experience design can redefine how business and design work together to create value in more efficient ways that also help business be more nimble and proactive in negotiating change.

The frameworks we will present next can help any organization be more effective in engaging customers around value and getting more out of the collaboration between business and design. This shift has already started, and we encourage businesses of all types and scale to begin to ask how can they start to take small steps to make better outcomes.

Section II
Frameworks and Tools

Give a man a fish
and you feed him for a day.
Teach a man to fish
and you feed him for a lifetime.

—Chinese Proverb[1]

A variation of the teach-a-man-to-fish concept could also be to buy the cookbooks put out by the eating establishments you like to frequent and then try to make the same dishes at home, with the hope that you can cut down on your restaurant expenses. But having a recipe doesn't make you a chef, and not all recipes in a given book are exactly how the chef prepares his or her version. What you can learn from a good cookbook is a bit about the cuisine and the role that different ingredients play in creating its characteristic flavors. You can also get an overview of the approach, basic techniques, and patterns, all of which can save you time or allow you to experiment a bit for yourself.

Is it wise to teach others your trade? What if the person is a potential customer? A competitor? There's an interesting case study from the field of supply-chain management in which the supplier kept encouraging its customers to outsource new aspects of its product. Essentially, the supplier was willing to try to reduce costs for the company in the new areas and was willing to take on the risk of learning. Eventually the company allowed the supplier to attempt to provide all the main components of the product at the company's accepted quality standards. The supplier quickly became one of the company's strongest competitors, as they were able to take the knowledge they had developed, combined with their strengths as a supplier, to introduce a product into the market that was of similar quality but cost less than the original company's product.

There are reasons why intellectual property is a field of law and why trademarks and trade dress play an important role in modern economies. There is also the human ability to derive meaning and knowledge from observation and to create new value without necessarily violating anyone else's legal claims on that which had been observed.

Because experience design touches on many aspects and areas that already exist in the collaboration between business and design, it's understandable that some may consider current processes to be close enough or assume that they're already doing it. To help illustrate what's different and to make experience design more accessible for a larger set of minds to consider, discuss, and help move forward, we will share some of the basics in this section.

As we stated at the start of this book, we've decided that case studies are not the most effective approach to illustrating our take on experience design. Case studies become dated, or if circumstances change, the outcome may prove to be unsuccessful. Or people may jump to the conclusion that their situation is close or different enough that they can simply assume that a view applies or doesn't apply without really thinking things all the way through. There's also the point that, although some may think that what we present is common sense, common sense is not as common as people might assume it to be. To that end, we would rather share more details to help strengthen the understanding and resonance of our point and hope that others can benefit.

This section will present frameworks and tools that we have either created or found and, to some extent, refined through the course of business over the past 15 years. We believe that these are basic enough to not be trade secrets that we can't live without, but we also believe that they have enough value to be useful to others who are interested in integrating brand, value, and experience. If nothing else, we think that they will help business and design have more informed and intelligent discussions about how to collaborate.

5

Brand Frameworks and Tools

A brand is a living entity—and it is enriched or undermined cumulatively over time, the product of a thousand small gestures.

—Michael Eisner[1]

We believe that bringing a business's Brand to life through the products, services, and experiences customers have with the business is an important component of experience design and actually differentiates it from other user-centered design methodologies. One of the biggest challenges that both business and design face, however, is that a Brand is seldom defined with a real eye toward the actual experiences customers will have related to value. Brands have traditionally been developed with the goal of expression and have focused on developing a distinctive identity and communicating meaning through visuals and words. Another challenge is that Brand tends to be managed within a marketing function of a business and the emphasis is on visual consistency applied to tactical messaging based on specific business goals (building awareness, driving lead generation and demand, fueling sales, etc.).

There are two very common circumstances that we have seen when business and design come together at a strategic level around Brand. The first is when a start-up has an executive who tasks his or her design agency to help develop a world-class Brand before there is any substantive product, service, or customer base. We understand that executives want a high-quality Brand identity system, but it begins to position the Brand as just that—the visuals—and it does not address the experience component that makes the Brand real.

A second common circumstance is when a new person is brought in to run the marketing function of an existing business, and that person has a strategic objective to breathe new life or meaning into the Brand. Although it's natural for one to want to have an impact through one's position, it's important to understand what the current position of the Brand is and what really can and should be done to reflect changes in value for the customer. The risk is that the only real change that gets made is a new visual identity for the Brand, while the value (products, services, and customer experience) hasn't really changed.

We believe that too often Brand is equated with Branding. The problem is that the efforts involved in defining a visual and verbal refresh of a Brand don't necessarily address the Brand's role in defining real value or experience. For the purpose of experience design, we would like to propose several frameworks to help unlock the Brand for use across all areas of the interface between business and customer.

We aren't going to go into the basics of Brand, because the topic is already well covered in other books. But if you are looking for a solid foundation, we suggest reading *Strategic Brand Management* by Kevin Lane Keller[2] and *Building Strong Brands* by David Aaker.[3]

Brand Basics for Experience Design

For experience design, we are primarily interested in two things:

Brand concept or essence: There are several different names used, but the basic premise is that there is some underlying idea that is important to the business and to the customer that relates to the kind of value the business creates and how it relates to customer needs and perceptions. Regardless of what it's called, it's an important aspect for any Brand, but it's also essential for taking an experience design–centric approach because this should function as a guide for developing value.

Brand attributes: These are qualities that help characterize the Brand as it's expressed through touch points between the business and customers. They should also be applied to the qualities of interaction that anyone (including employees and partners) has with the Brand.

There are different approaches to developing Brand attributes, but the key point in relation to Brand experience is that a Brand relies on multiple attributes but not all attributes get equally used in bringing the Brand to life through customer experiences around value. This is because of the nature of words and how words function when used in a descriptive or prescriptive way.

For our purposes, Brand concept and Brand attributes provide a firm foundation for building and differentiating experiences that engage customers around value. As we discussed in the previous chapter, the *why* of value for a customer and the *how* of value delivery are questions that must always be answered when business and design are collaborating. To put it simply, the Brand concept informs the why, and Brand attributes inform the how. Concept and attributes can also reinforce each other, but we suggest starting with the basic relationship first. Part of getting this right is to check the integrity of the Brand concept and attributes to ensure they're going to be useful and don't need further development.

Brand Concept Frameworks

We use two frameworks to ensure that the Brand concept and attributes have been thought through and can function as a solid foundation for use in experience design. These frameworks preexist our concept of experience design, but we frequently use them because they help us guide the Brand conversation in useful and meaningful ways.

The first framework is the Ansoff Growth Matrix. This particular matrix is often used in developing corporate strategy because it helps develop different areas of focus that have specific tactical implications for a company. Figure 5.1 shows a version of this matrix, and when used in strategy, the quadrants are usually labeled, starting in the upper left and moving clockwise, as market penetration, product development, diversification, and market development.

We suggest also using this matrix to review the Brand concept. (You can even apply and use the quadrant labels, if desired.) This will help you understand whether the Brand concept remains relevant and can be used in all the quadrants, assuming that each quadrant represents a specific scenario of how a company and customer set would be interacting given specific business goals and market environments that the business is likely to encounter. For example, if you are developing a Brand concept, assume that you will be starting out in the upper left quadrant. Now choose the next likely quadrant that you see your business plan leading you to and develop scenarios for what you plan to do to reach that goal, trying to describe what would be different from your current offering. You can then look at your Brand concept and ask if it seems to comfortably include the new requirements, in addition to the existing focus.

It's not important that you are planning to make the kind of moves your scenario implies immediately, but it is a good way to ensure that you have a Brand concept

Figure 5.1
The Ansoff Growth Matrix

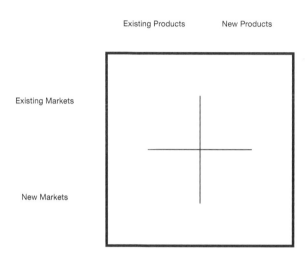

that is extensible. If it is, then it can be consistently used as a touchstone for evaluating the value you produce for customers and why they should care. If, however, it seems as if some highly probable scenarios will push the Brand concept to the breaking point, you should consider rethinking your Brand architecture (a framework we are about to present) so that future evolution does not come at the expense of the initial success you are creating.

The second Brand framework is a standard Brand architecture and value positioning matrix, as shown in Figure 5.2. *Brand architecture* refers to the relationship between Brands that a company owns and uses. The vertical axis of the matrix is a spectrum between two common approaches that businesses take—Branded house versus house of Brands (we believe this spectrum was first coined by David Aaker and Erich Joachimsthaler).

Each side of this spectrum has its own pros and cons depending on your business, industry, customer base, and so on, but our main point is that for your Brand concept to be an effective input for experience design, you need to determine how well it supports the kind of business and activities you intend to pursue. Failing to do this creates internal and external confusion and can become incredibly complex to manage and design for correctly. If you wind up with more than one Brand, it will be difficult to have them mean the same thing, and if you simply create Brands for different purposes, they won't necessarily have different experiences unless you can provide guidance for what is different about them.

Think about it like this: Through how many Brands will you represent your business activities and have the market (all potential consumers, not just customers) see and experience your actions? It is important to understand whether or not everything is going to be covered with one Brand or with several Brands. If it's the latter, you

Figure 5.2
Brand Architecture and Value Positioning Matrix

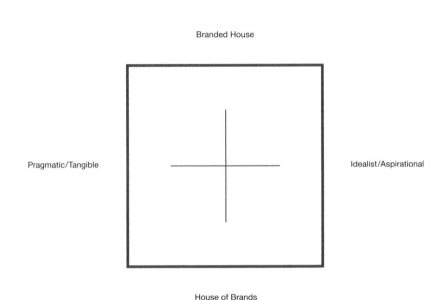

Branded House

Pragmatic/Tangible

Idealist/Aspirational

House of Brands

should be defining how these Brands are related, if at all, at a Brand concept level.

The horizontal axis of this framework speaks a bit more to the qualities the market should perceive when customers are experiencing the value the Brand delivers. In some ways this can be seen as either a roll-up of the Brand attributes or an important criterion for developing and prioritizing attributes. If you find that it makes the most sense for your Brand to be more Branded house or single Brand concept dominant, then you should decide which side of the overall value perception works best for the Brand concept. The more pragmatic and tangible the overall appeal of the Brand, the more limited the kind of value it can provide, as it always needs to reinforce the pragmatic and tangible aspects of the value. The more idealist and aspirational the appeal of the Brand, the more important it is to make sure that customers agree that the pragmatic and tangible value you provide leads to the idealistic and aspirational value they seek. It's much easier to prove a tangible, but having someone agree and believe in intangibles can be more powerful at driving certain kinds of behavior.

If you are a house of Brands, then each member Brand should have a clear intended value perception. Whether or not the member Brands' value perceptions relate to one another depends on whether or not a given customer is likely to buy more than one and how the value delivered from each relates to the others. It's not imperative that they relate in any way.

You can start with either of these frameworks and check how your thinking plays out across the other, but the main thing to do is consider your Brand through both of them to make sure that you have a clear understanding of the Brand concept and how singular or componentized across Brands it needs to be. Without a clear understanding, you will have difficulty talking about your Brand and how you will use it to create and deliver value.

These ways of looking at Brand concept are really just preparatory steps for using Brand to build value and engage customers. What's even more important than thinking about how your Brand concept maps to your business goals is making sure that you can connect the Brand concept to value for customers. This is where many conventional approaches to Brand stop short. Figure 4.4 in the previous chapter shows the downstream flow of intent from business to customer and the corresponding upstream flow of meaning from customer to business. This is the key area in which Brand concept needs to be considered. Why? Because this is what customers really care about, and if you do this right, we believe you can build a differentiated Brand.

Brand Concept to Real Value

Over the years, we've worked with many different clients and tried to help them understand the Brand-value connection. In our work with Nokia, specifically with Brian Kralyevich, we developed a framework for just this purpose. Kralyevich had worked in the design services field during the late 1990s in San Francisco and then had become a client of ours when he was at Microsoft, where he was involved with Windows, Zune, and Xbox. When he was at Nokia, he was helping the product company begin to focus on designing services. As we worked with his group, he related the concept of Red Threads—design principles—that they used in his teams at Microsoft. The idea was that a universal design principle could be something that teams could use as a guide and an objective in various design efforts and that, if effectively achieved, could unify the experience for end users. We proposed taking this idea a step further using a similar approach—but instead of design principles, we suggested translating the Brand concept into a set of Brand value pillars that are value proposition categories or themes that would inform service development. This would help designers approach developing new services in a way that ensured that the experiences people had with the services reinforced the Brand's position and meaning.

The concept rests on three simple levels. Figure 5.3 shows how these levels work. The first is the Brand concept, which can be taken as is or, using the processes outlined earlier, refined to align against emerging opportunities or changes in the business. The next level is the Brand value pillars. These are categories that define the types of value propositions that relate to the Brand concept but generally describe how a customer gets value at a high level. It's essentially describing a class of products or services that would take the idea embodied in the Brand concept and turn it into real value for people. A Brand concept can have multiple Brand value pillars, but each should be fairly distinct from the others and it should be clear why they are different.

The next level would be made up of specific ways of bringing this value to reality and to customers, either through features, entire products, or services. Each Brand value pillar could have multiple examples of real value. The only requirement is that each example must articulate true benefits through value (either tangible, intangible, or aspirational) and through outcomes that would make a difference for customers (ways of thinking, emotions, or actions).

The purpose of such an approach is twofold. The first is it moves the discussion away from high-level Brand concepts that no one can really disagree with as being good but that no one really uses in decision making on a strategic or tactical level. The second is to build a mechanism for exploring decisions around the development, design, and delivery of value through products and services that can be used to ensure that the outcomes support the Brand and aren't random or driven by shortsighted efficiency needs. It also helps business and design move away from simply evaluating design outcomes based on appearance and allows them to examine how effective an approach is at delivering Brand value.

The Brand concept, a singular idea, can rest on multiple Brand value pillars, and each of these can be made real in multiple ways. Think of it this way—many people develop a spiritual or religious affiliation. A Brand concept is analogous to the basic underlying belief of a spiritual belief or religion. All religions have tenets or principles that people who believe agree to follow and use to guide their actions; Brand value pillars are the analogy of these tenets. The features, products, and services are roughly equivalent to the practices, acts, and deeds one does in compliance with these tenets to bring the spiritual or religious belief into daily living. We aren't trying to equate Brands with religions; we are just using the example to make a point (although business leaders might enjoy the thought of Brand tithing). Making Brand actionable through concepts such as Brand value pillars (or whatever you would like to call them) provides some very useful benefits. It creates a framework of multiple value-based criteria that can be used to inform product and service development and help guide and prioritize how value is made real for customers. It also allows for the weaving of different variations of Brand concept–related value to be used within a product or service, helping diversify and differentiate product and service offerings. But perhaps one of the most interesting aspects of this framework is that it also allows the Brand concept to be reinterpreted into different kinds of value as changes in the business environment arise. It can function as a Brand's DNA for future evolution and can become a way to investigate new areas in which sustaining, down-market and disruptive innovation can be researched and developed.

We hope that readers are able to see how something such as the Brand value pillars tool can be used to inform the *why* of a project. In conjunction with the Brand concept, it can be used to help ideate features and opportunities and to prioritize requirements in a way that differentiates a product or service from those of competitors. What we think is so powerful about this is that it's not placing any "design" stakes in the ground but is focused on what is valuable to the customer. In this way it helps bring the Brand out of the visual guideline police role and gives it an active role in delivering value. That having been said, there's one other framework that should be used with it—one that helps bring the Brand to life by answering how.

Figure 5.3
Brand Value Pillars Framework for Translating
Brand Concept into Customer Value

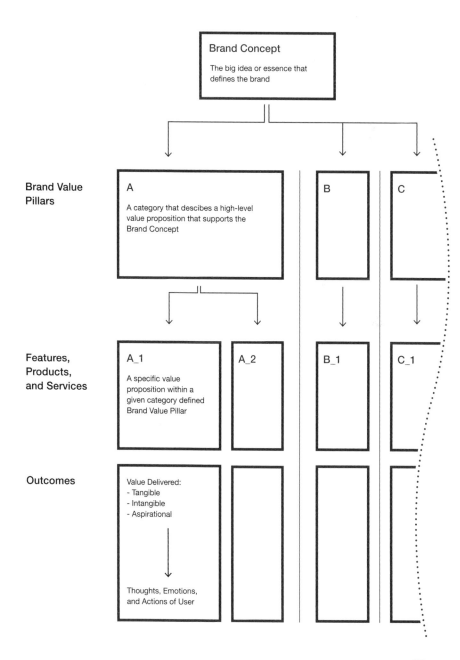

Brand Attribute Framework

Brand attributes are qualities that help differentiate Brands and that are often used as criteria for developing and evaluating design outcomes used in the expression of Brands. Often, Brand attributes are listed in Brand guidelines, usually with some context as to why they are important for the Brand, but that's it. They rarely get used on an ongoing basis.

While working at another studio many years ago, we were involved in a project that was intended to develop the Brand and user interface for a software product that would provide an innovative way for venture capitalists to collaborate while evaluating prospective investment opportunities. The project director led the client team and the design team on a thoroughly engaging process of developing different approaches to what the personality of the Brand might be. It culminated with a work session in which four personas were revealed, each being a potential representative of what the brand character was like. Each one was based on a real or fictional character that the collective teams had discussed and decided were relevant. In addition to bringing the personas to life visually, there were additional terms—attributes—about the Brand and product that had come out of discussions in the preceding weeks. These terms had been grouped to enhance specific personas, and the discussion was lively as everyone talked about their favorite persona and why they liked it.

When it was time to choose the right persona for the Brand, it was a relatively simple process; two stood out as the most appropriate, but one was perhaps too conservative for the company and its innovative product. A winner was chosen. The chief executive officer of the company said to our project lead, "Boy, this was fun! Also seems like it took a lot of time to do all this. So how does this inform our Brand and our product interface?"

That's where things came to a stop. The project director had done a great job of teasing out relevant attributes in a way that was entertaining and creative, but they didn't have an effective strategy for how to use the attributes. We say "effective strategy" since the project director had assumed that it would be self-evident how to apply the attributes to the Brand. But there were two problems: (1) Some of the attributes seemed to challenge each other, and it was unclear how we would prioritize them for the Brand; and (2) it was unclear how the attributes would inform the user interface of the product.

This is when the next framework was born. We realized that not all attributes are created equally. Many of the attributes were semantically or conceptually related, and one could categorize them into meta-attributes that contained or relied on individual attributes. Not all attributes could or should be applied equally. For instance, it's a lot easier to visualize "modern" or "friendly" than it is "innovative" or "efficient." We also realized that things such as "efficient" and "smooth" might be more powerful when applied to behaviors (transitions, or the way a tool works) than simply conveyed through colors, shapes, or font choices.

Figure 5.4 shows the Brand attribute framework. The purpose of this framework is to help identify what the purpose of an attribute really is and to help make it more effective as a criterion for developing and evaluating experiences customers have with a Brand. Although this can be used during the development of a Brand, it can also be used with existing attributes or to help establish attributes that speak to certain areas of experience that may not have originally been considered when the Brand was developed.

Figure 5.4
Brand Attribute Matrix:
List and Applications

Applications and Uses	Primary Attribute A	Secondary Attributes A1 A2		Primar Attribui B
Description and Examples				
Symbol				
Sound				
Typography				
Photography — - Style - Composition - Content				
Graphic Forms				
Color				
Materials				
Language — - Tone - Vocabulary				
Movement — - Speed - Physics - Transitions - Dimensionality - Size shift - Translucency - Lighting/shading				

There are several steps to using this framework, but the first is to simply group the attributes into categories of similarity or relatedness (for instance, "integrity" might include terms like credible, trustworthy, and reliable). The purpose of this is to reduce the number of main attributes to a manageable number; we usually suggest three to five meta-attributes.

The next step is to list the attributes hierarchically and then add a brief description of how the words should be interpreted. These descriptions can be enriched through examples—references, photos, or other elements—that help to clarify the descriptions. This can be important, because what *modern* means to one person may differ from another's vision of it. Or in some cases, a reference to a sound, an object, or the way something moves or feels will be the best description. The goal is to bring the attribute to life in a way that makes the most sense for those who chose it as being relevant for the Brand.

Then, based on the literal and added meaning of the word, look at the overall experience matrix and decide where the attribute can most effectively be used. It's not important that each attribute work in every experience "cell," and it would be surprising if many did. What's important is to be clear about how an attribute should be considered, based on the areas of the experience to which it applies. The degree of detail in defining the experience cells can vary, but we have presented what we believe are important basics. It's also important to consider how the Brand personality will be positioned and what kinds of products, services, and touch points will be experienced by customers. You don't need to populate experience cells that will have no relevance to the customer's experience of the Brand. Conversely, you want to make sure you identify and describe ones that will be very important.

Note that you may map your Brand this way and realize that there are a lot of areas of experience for which you have no attributes to apply. This is exactly the problem with many current approaches to Branding—they happen in a bit of a vacuum and don't really anticipate what the Brand is going to need to accomplish. It's also to see how easy it is to not apply the Brand, beyond application of a logo and color to product and service experiences, especially if no one has thought about how the Brand should be brought to life. It's possible to update this kind of matrix based on design outcomes that happen to be successful and seem to embody the Brand, even though it was largely the result of an inspired creative team and not necessarily based on inputs to the design process. Ideally, this kind of attribute matrix would become an additional section of the Brand guidelines.

We will close this chapter with one last point, and that is to illustrate how the Brand value pillars and Brand attributes matrix can be used in concert to help guide a product or service development effort (we will delve further into this in the next chapter). Our purpose here is simply to show how focusing on the Brand can bring a more Brand-centric approach to answering the *why* and *how* when business and design collaborate.

Figure 5.5 shows how Brand attributes are used to help determine how a given Brand value pillar is used to create value in a way that reinforces the qualities of the experience a customer has in perceiving value delivered by the Brand. As business and design explore the actual processes and stages of engagement at a touch point, decisions about the actual techniques used can be evaluated against which attributes enhance the value and communicate the unique character of the Brand.

Figure 5.5
Using Brand Value Pillars and an Attribute
Matrix to Develop Touch Points

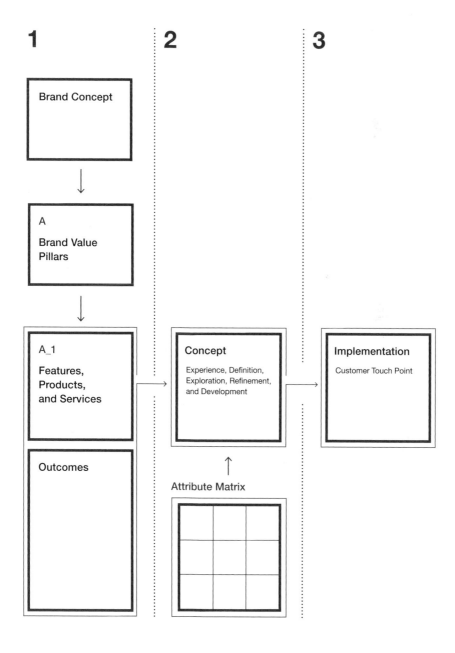

1

Brand Concept

A

Brand Value
Pillars

A_1

Features,
Products,
and Services

Outcomes

2

Concept

Experience, Definition,
Exploration, Refinement,
and Development

Attribute Matrix

3

Implementation

Customer Touch Point

Perhaps one of the most important aspects of using the Brand beyond the surface of experiences is realizing that Brand value pillars and attributes should be applied to the entire customer journey, not just to products and services, as a means to identify levels of engagement before, during, and after the customer has bought from the business. The categories of value embodied in the Brand value pillars can act as a foundation for developing a range of initiatives that deliver value and give customers a reason to interact with the Brand. We will delve into this in more detail in Chapter 7 as we discuss the customer journey framework.

6

Product/Service Frameworks and Tools

Prediction seems to defy a Law of Nature: You cannot see the future because it is not here yet. We find a work-around by building machines that learn from experience. It's the regimented discipline of using what we do know—in the form of data—to place increasingly accurate odds on what's coming next.

—Eric Siegel, *Predictive Analytics*[1]

In general, our ability to predict outcomes for situations involving people is increasing within certain contexts. This is due largely to the fact that we now have vast amounts of data and the computing power and methodologies to efficiently mine these data for patterns and implications. However, at the time we are writing this, we are unaware of a process for accurately predicting what people will find valuable in the future. Once a need is identified, finding a solution that fills it is much easier. Necessity is the mother of invention.

Yet there is still a bit of skill involved in meeting an identified need in a way that is efficient, sustainable (environmentally and economically), and willingly adopted by people. And this is the area in which business and design so often find themselves collaborating, because it is here that value can be developed (and on which the entire premise of a business rests).

The human mind—the natural computer/the inherent designer—is very adept at processing large amounts of data and using this to build predictive models, but it also has limitations. It cannot fully analyze large amounts of data, so the patterns and connections it can see may be illusions or be more correlative than causal. It is not truly rational and cannot even know for sure when it has departed rational analysis and entered into biased interpretations. Although these are serious limitations, the human mind also has one huge benefit that current computing technology doesn't provide: It uses insights to make connections that can lead to innovations.

Products, services, and solutions are the reasons that customers interact with businesses and are the basis of any real value exchange that allows the business to exist. As such, they are also a very important component of the overall experience that customers have with a business and Brand. It's where the rubber meets the road. If there's no value here, there's no value in the relationship.

Taking an experience design approach to developing products and services helps prevent the mistake of assuming that a feature or technology is the same thing as value. Business often comes to the table with a list of specific requirements and a request for design to make the product or service successful by creating a compelling experience for the customer. The challenge is, if that compelling experience is the only value that the product or service really delivers, the customer may not engage with it for very long.

The approach we recommend is to make sure that you have the right information to fully understand the customer context and think through the real areas of need and opportunity. Next, select those that create real value for the customer and reinforce the intention of the Brand. Then think about how the product or service and customer relationship are likely to change over time.

The process of understanding true needs and thinking through context and future needs is not trivial; we will be sharing quite a bit of thinking. To make this a little easier, we have divided this chapter into three parts that roughly correspond to initial thinking and definition, a more extended view of what can change across the product life cycle, and finally, how to react to outside change.

Part 1
Initial Thinking and Definition

Too often, the lack of rationality that comes along with the way we are wired allows us to move full steam ahead with ideas for products and services that are not quite right. With more effort, we could easily avoid mistakes, reduce extraneous efforts that might prove to be of no value, and even find better ideas that are more valuable than the original idea. In *Thinking, Fast and Slow*, Daniel Kahneman describes several of these shortcomings, including WYSIATI, or what you see is all there is (that is, the information that you have is all that there really is, so there's no point in looking for more), and confirmation bias, or the tendency for people to "seek data that are likely to be compatible with the beliefs that they already hold."[2] There is also an inverse to confirmation bias, which Samuel Arbesman in *Half-Life of Facts* describes as the Semmelweis reflex, where there is a tendency to invalidate or ignore information that is counter to what we believe. (It is named after Ignaz Semmelweis, who was ostracized for suggesting that the death of mothers after childbirth was related to their obstetricians performing deliveries immediately after performing autopsies. Semmelweis believed that these doctors who were "going directly from the morgue to the delivery room" were spreading infections "from the cadavers to the women giving birth, leading to their deaths," a proposition that outraged his peers.[3])

Starting with the Right Information

You can't truly adhere to the principles of experience design or work with its core components unless you have the right amount and kind of information. You don't need to have all the answers at the very beginning, but you have to be increasing your area of consideration and making informed decisions. Deciding that you don't need some information or that you are comfortable making subjective decisions or leaving issues for later consideration can compromise the effectiveness of an experience design approach.

All the frameworks and tools we will share in this chapter have one thing in common: They will be more effective when used in conjunction with a good supply of information. This includes an understanding of the future versions on the product/service road map, their likelihood of occurring, and their interdependence on the features of the current version. It also includes how and where the product or service will be first encountered and eventually accessed by users (marketing and sales channels, channel partners, distributors and retailers, and third-party service providers), what additional variations and complementary products or services might be offered, and how these would integrate into or enhance the existing version (including platform specific variations and third-party add-ons). Details of the business model, such as cost, ownership model, warranty, licensing agreement, and support, are important, too.

We aren't alone in the belief that early information is a key to success. Most current design methodologies are based on how information can be used more effectively and earlier in the process. *The Wide Lens* is based on the concept that innovation occurs in the context of a larger network of suppliers and adopters, and that not having the right information (and acting accordingly) is what leads to failure. There are several case studies of billion-dollar investments that became failures because the right information (though readily available) wasn't considered. In *The Wide Lens*, Ron Adner relates the story of the development of inhalable insulin, a breathtaking example of how a well-thought-out product was felled by lack of adequate information. The business leaders did all the right things and followed all the best practices they could possibly think of, yet they failed to explore what actually happens in one small part of the customer experience. They assumed that because they had accounted for the step in the process, that they were well prepared to proceed. The point in question was that for a patient to use and benefit from an inhalable version of insulin, he or she had to have the respiratory capability to use the product. All that the patient needed to receive a prescription from a doctor was approval from a specialist. What the business didn't account for was how this would actually happen, and that it was in fact a bottleneck that jeopardized everything they were doing beyond repair. The number of respiratory specialists was so small that there was a six-month wait for appointments. Because no newly diagnosed diabetic can wait that long to start insulin treatment, patients had no choice but to use standard products, and the likelihood of switching was too small to sustain the business investment made behind the development, marketing, and distribution of the inhalable product.[4]

Not every omission of information will have that kind of impact, but we are always surprised to see what kinds of assumptions are brought to the table that clearly have not been based on an understanding of real people in the real world.

The primary area of information that should be accessible for experience design is information about the customer. This is also an area in which the process can get off on the wrong foot quickly. Several problems can occur when trying to describe the customer. The first and most common is that the business (or design team) assumes it accurately represents the customer. This can be true only if the product or service is to be sold to businesses and design teams. When it seems as though decisions are being made based on this assumption, the first questions to ask are: Are we really going to buy or use this? Does success depend on our financial commitment to using the product and service? If the answer to these is no, then the team should be very careful about thinking that they can or should represent the customer.

A second mistake is that a customer segmentation model used in marketing becomes the basis for describing actual customer needs. These segmentation models can be useful in identifying certain relationships between demographics, psychographics, values, and preferred channels of engagement, but they may be of very little use in determining what will be valuable in a product or service. Although they may be useful in understanding how someone thinks about value, very rarely will they be truly useful in determining what is valuable. As an example, we have often been asked to recruit market research groups based on segmentation models. Each group representing a segment is then shown the same product, which fulfills a basic function—for instance, a mobile camera. Then the client asks for an analysis of which features are more desirable to which segments. The reality is that if all segments have the same basic need, then all the functions necessary for fulfilling the need are seen as valuable; nothing stands out. This is because the need is defined by a horizontal microsegment that cuts across the main segmentation model. In these situations, the importance of the microsegment becomes more important than the macrosegmentation. If the basic needs do not vary by segment and only the circumstance and context of the segment vary, then the model will not be extremely useful. Conversely, if there is a need that does cut across all segments (say, ease of use), then the need can be important to the product or service development effort even if the segmentation model isn't. Now, we aren't saying that experience design doesn't take people into account—an understanding of the actual customer is hugely important. However, we recommend taking an a priori segmentation model with many grains of salt.

Another common mistake that occurs when defining technology-based services is assuming that the world is flat. By this, we mean assuming that everything is the same for everyone everywhere. Many times the business or design team is located in or near an urban center that has a fairly high degree of technology adoption and service penetration. This can lead to assumptions about the degree of familiarity about technology that aren't true in other regions (although this is changing) and to assumptions about what people find value in that may not be true. For example, even if everyone in a rural community has broadband mobile devices and is active on Facebook, location-based couponing still may not make a lot of sense because the nearest place to receive or redeem a coupon may be miles away.

This raises the question, How do you get a real picture of the customer? The simple answer is to create a well-thought-out research plan that can provide the right observation, analysis, and insight development. This can be done in very lightweight, guerrilla-style efforts or through very rigorous and broadly conducted programs that include ethnographic techniques, design analysis, qualitative interviews, quantitative surveys and testing, persona development, participatory design programs, and detailed usability testing. The MVP (minimum viable product) philosophy suggests that getting real customers by using a minimal but real version of the product is the best approach, because you commit to less, learn more based on real-world use, and often generate some level of revenue. In some cases this isn't possible because a product is too complex, requires levels of internal or external approval before being introduced to the market, or is required by the Brand to achieve a certain level of quality to maintain its meaning and integrity. The point is that the means should justify the ends: You need to understand what you want to know and develop the right programs to provide the information that will be of the highest use. The first question to ask is: Are we looking broadly enough for more information? If the answer to that is yes, then the next question is: How can we be sure?

We find that businesses, by their own admission, often come to the table with an incomplete understanding of the customer. They may have done some research or outreach, but they often say that they hope we can help develop a more complete picture for them.

In general, experience design is concerned with three kinds of needs: existing, unmet, and emerging. Some are often easier to identify and validate because you can ask people what they need, whereas others come to light only through observation and analysis. Here's the catch: People are not rational, and what they say they do and need is often very different from what really happens and what would be of most use. The challenge is to balance the information gathering to give you as much data and analysis for surfacing the best insights in the time frame and budget available to the team.

Paul Valerio, a principal at Method, leads our Insights practice. He has spent many years helping businesses and designers get the right information about customers so that they can understand what problems are really worth solving. He recommends the following approaches for gaining more insights about customers.

Qualitative Approaches

These research techniques are aimed at identifying contextual and narrative elements that are preserved through the observation of how target audience respondents behave and how they communicate when they discuss their interaction with a product or service category. It's not just what happens and what respondents say about it, but where and when it happened, next to what, before and after what, how respondents described it, and what else respondents were doing while it was happening and they were talking about it.

The value of qualitative methods is the deeper understanding they can generate about the interaction between rational and emotional motivations, the inclusion of externalities that can influence behavior, and the opportunity they afford human observers to capture the intangible elements of an environment that standardized data collection methodologies (surveys, self-administered customer ratings, etc.) cannot. These include:

Ethnography: This is an immersion technique in which researchers observe and follow a respondent as the person performs a given task being studied over a continuous stretch of time, from hours to days or longer. This can be done by means of in-person visits (one long visit or a series of visits) or with the respondent providing detailed diary-type reports. Although time- and money-intensive to conduct, the benefit is that a particularly rich set of contexts, adjacencies, and motivations can be encountered in a relatively short period of time, thus allowing insights to be generated across a wide set of potential dimensions, both directly and indirectly related to a specific topic.

In-home/on-site interview: A shorter, more concise, and focused approach, this type of interview has the same goals as an ethnographic study but takes place within a single location. The interview format is simply taken into the respondent's own context, instead of both members meeting at a neutral site such as a market research facility. This type of interview provides a good balance between efficiency and depth, because several interviews can be completed per day while still allowing for some contextual input.

Online bulletin board/forum: Usually text-based and occasionally image- or video-based, this approach still can generate useful input in the form of natural consumer language and perspectives, with quick turnaround and broad geographic reach. The forums can be moderated either formally or informally, so the discussions can be guided toward specific key topics, or allowed to meander according to the natural paths of the respondents.

Focus group: Although drawbacks include cost and time to plan, recruit, conduct, and analyze the findings, there is still value in conducting group discussions among target audience respondents when the topic and project timing permit. Focus groups are best used to understand how a specific product area is discussed, rather than as an evaluative tool for concepts. Focus groups do not function well as a batch approach to individual interviews. This is because the conversational format is ideal for observing how respondents do or do not influence one another in the course of a discussion among peers; for evaluative purposes, this format is often counterproductive.

Quantitative Approaches

Although not as widely used for experience research, used correctly quantitative research can provide data that qualitative research cannot, thus creating a more complete set of data for generating deeper understanding of complex user experiences.

The main path to these insights is through the revealing of patterns of perception that are invisible to qualitative methods, patterns that are not evident in a single respondent but that can be shown to be shared or divisive across otherwise similarly defined target audience segments. The main method used is:

> Survey research: Almost all quantitative survey research is now conducted via online questionnaires, although in-person interviews can still be done when security concerns or product prototype interactions need to be addressed. In either case, a standardized questionnaire format is used with minimal, if any, direct guidance or discussion coming from the interviewer.

Valerio points out that quantitative research can be statistically valid and can be used for projection, whereas qualitative is typically not statistically valid. However, he also points out that qualitative research often provides more meaningful insights because you are seeing real people in situ in the context that you are trying to learn about.

After a sound understanding of the customer, the other main area of information needed for experience design is the broader context in which the product or service will exist. There are many great sources for what kinds of research can be done and how to do it, so here we only quickly list some that are low-hanging fruit and that can be scaled to meet most needs.

These efforts do not always require a quantitative approach, but if the groups you need to learn from are of a certain scale and importance to the success of the product or service, it may be worth considering getting the right level of statistical validation. We recommend at least having initial conversations or cursory fact-finding efforts with the following:

> Internal stakeholders: Two levels of internal stakeholders should be considered when looking to gain information for products and services. The first are those who have a direct knowledge about the business model, competitive space, nature of the customer, and strengths and weaknesses of the company. The second are those who have knowledge about the upstream and downstream stages (such as marketing and customer support) and parallel business functions (such as billing and partner relations). The inputs should also be weighed against the stakeholder's connection to the product or service. (Does its success help the stakeholder and his or her career or make things more difficult?)

> External partners: Suppliers, buyers, channel partners, distributors, retailers, third-party developers, and service providers—all these groups

will have a perspective on what a business is doing, where the value is strongest and weakest, and what is changing in the overall value chain. In addition, those who have a view of the customer will also have an opinion about what customers perceive as value but that is not fully considered by the business providing the original product or service. It is also important to understand the nature of the relationship between the business and the partner, because this will color the person's perspective.

Analysts and experts: This includes people who cover the business or the industry for investors or for the press—people who have spent a lot of time in a particular field. These sources can provide larger contexts for what long-term success would entail, as well as an external view on competition and industry or sector dynamics. They can also help surface important historical issues or current efforts that can inform an understanding of the context within which a product or service exists.

Audits or design analysis of existing products and services: By examining an existing product or service experience, an audit can simply focus on what is going on at different stages, with brief descriptions and perhaps opinions on the quality of the experience. A design analysis would focus more on how specific aspects of the design played a role in the overall tangible, intangible, and aspirational value of the product or service; which elements were most important; which might be improved upon; and which seemed extraneous.

Secondary research: This entails reviewing research, commentary, and analyses published by others. The Internet is the obvious source for doing initial quick reviews to see what relevant information exists and to identify how others look at a particular opportunity space.

Figure 6.1 is a general schematic for the kinds of information gathering that help to provide an experience design–centric approach to product and service development.

There are four main stages: initial context setting, in which the focus is on making sure the right questions have been asked and the best information is available; mid-stage course correction, in which the "measure twice, cut once" rule becomes important to practice, along with the validation of assumptions and checking for interdependencies can occur; the prerelease, in which the obvious errors are identified; and finally the "how did we do?" stage, in which understanding the gap between intent and reality can be assessed.

Figure 6.1
Stages of Information Gathering

Stage	Activities
Initial Context Setting	- Qualitative Research - Quantitative Research - Fact-finding Efforts
Mid-Stage Course Correcting	- Concept Validation - Participatory Design - Cross-functional - Proof of Concept Sharing - Early Customer and Partner Demos
Prerelease	- Professional QA - Usability Testing - Alpha/Beta-Testing - Customer and Partner Demos
How Did We Do?	- Call Center/Support Audits - User Groups - Customer Interviews - Press Coverage Audits

Frameworks

We want to introduce three frameworks. The first is useful for start-ups, or new products and services, but can also help with existing product or service extension and evolution. The second is useful for extending and evolving existing products and services, especially with an eye for touch point ecosystems. The third is useful for reacting to external change: deciding whether or not existing value can be extended and evolved, whether or not new value is needed, and how this plays into existing value.

Figure 6.2
Needs and Value Framework

Customer/Role Name

	A	B	C	D
Description				
Priority Ranking				
Pain Points				
Needs				
Value Propositions				
Proof Points				

Needs and Value Propositions Framework

This framework has a bit of overlap with many basic product management methodologies, but it's also a way to use the Brand as a tool set for increasing and differentiating products and services while still answering the question: Why would a customer see the product or service as valuable? Figure 6.2 is a standard version of the framework we often use. It can be modified as needed.

This exercise begins with identification of the customer. Specifically, the first step is to identify the different roles a customer may have, such as buyer, user, account holder, and so forth. In many business-to-business situations, these may include departmental descriptions and levels: such as the role they play in the decision-making/purchase process. The important point is to begin with as many potential customers that could potentially be relevant. (It's also worth noting that in the case of technology products and services, there may also be partners or third parties that should be considered. Although they may not pay to use the product or service, they may play a role in delivering value to end users, and there may need to be an acknowledgment of what needs they have and what value they expect in order to play their expected parts.)

Once an initial list of customer roles is developed, the next step is to fill in what is known about the customers' pain points and needs that are going to be addressed by the proposed product or service or that are relevant to customers' use of the product or service. There doesn't need to be a one-to-one correspondence between pain points and needs, but it is useful to understand why a need exists and if there are current circumstances that make meeting a need more important or more difficult. It is also useful to know how needs that may be shared across different customers may have very different pain points, because this could affect how a customer perceives value.

Once this level of the framework has been completed, the next task is to prioritize customers by importance. Different attributes can be used here, but several good ones include role in purchase decision, amount of use, size of need, importance of need, and importance of use and adoption. The main goal is to understand which customers might be more important and why. Because needs may be divergent or there may need to be a staging of product or service capabilities, it's helpful to understand which customers' needs should be prioritized.

There may also be opportunities to collapse multiple customers into a single group if their pain points and needs are largely the same, although it should still be understood that their usage patterns may differ, which may affect how the "meta-customer" is prioritized.

When everyone on the team has a basic understanding of the customer's pain points and needs, they can begin to identify value propositions that meet those needs. This is where the Brand value pillars can be of use in helping bring a Brand-differentiated approach to thinking about value.

One common mistake that happens at this point is to confuse value propositions, or proof points, with requirements or features. We suggest that at this stage, value propositions be worded as benefit statements, describing the benefit of the outcome and speaking to the fulfillment of needs. For example, instead of saying that a music service provides recommendations based on a listener's previous choices, you might say, "Makes it easier for people to discover new music that they will like without spending lots of time listening to options that they don't like." This allows for an exploration of how different value propositions can be supported by the same requirement or feature without jumping to a conclusion about how to provide the value. Too often, product requirements and features are derived from a one-to-one correspondence to a need, which could result in missing innovative approaches or having too many features and an overly complex user experience.

After the value propositions have been articulated, there can be an exercise to refine and/or consolidate. Whether or not you do this, we recommend the addition of proof points that customers would need or expect to see in order to agree that the product or service could actually meet their needs.

This framework provides multiple benefits in ensuring that efforts translate to customer value and reinforce Brand meaning. It can ensure that there will be value for customers and that the team knows what that value will be and can account for it by mapping value to features during design, development, and testing. It can help product managers better understand how to prioritize the value that a product or service will provide and enable the Brand to influence the approach before all the decisions about what the product or service is going to be have been made.

This framework is most effective when used during early planning stages of product or service definition. It can be filled out in one session or iteratively using initial assumptions and then updating based on research results and analysis. It can also be used when a project has lost its way and managers need to figure out the most important areas to focus their efforts on and prioritize resource allocation. The framework can also be used to inform marketing and message development, because it can provide a good outline of the kinds of benefits a product or service can deliver. It can also be used to evaluate the effectiveness of design decisions, especially when analyzing support questions and requests.

One question that is bound to arise is how this framework and experience design for products and services differs from product management. In our experience, good product managers tend to have one or more potential experience background: sales/marketing, engineering/technical production, project management, subject matter expertise, or business management. Frequently, they may combine a number of these but are strongest in one field that aligns with the overall product and business culture in which they work. The common theme that all product managers should bring to the table is an understanding of the customer, what the customer's needs are and what they find valuable, and the overall process for creating the product or service. The best product managers, based on our interactions, are the ones who keep value for the customer as the imperative and prioritize trade-offs based on maximizing value. But what product managers do not necessarily bring to the process are the additional systems thinking perspectives that keep the effort from becoming a separate silo of activity within the business. These additional perspectives include Brand as input to the why and how of value, cross-functional focus across other products and services that the customer may buy or use from the same company, and a full pre-sales and post-sales customer experience model beyond the specific product road map.

Product management is often focused on maintaining velocity against road map milestones while maintaining quality and value for the customer. Experience design is a way to make sure that the Brand informs thinking in meaningful ways and that the design decisions take into account the other areas of experience—either as influence and leverage or by informing them with new opportunities through which to engage the customer. Furthermore, experience design can also help the entire process leverage the skills and benefits of the craft of design based on the different disciplines involved by ensuring that the how reinforces the characteristics of the Brand while enhancing value for the customer, and not just being "artifice." To this end, we suggest that this framework be used in conjunction with the Brand frameworks during the early stages of the product or service definition.

Context and Ecosystem Frameworks

This second framework broadens the perspective beyond the given product or service by considering variations in the customer context, as well as variations of needs across different platforms.

We defined products, services, and solutions in Chapter 2, and one of the things that can happen as technology becomes a larger component of both underlying functionality and customer value is that products begin to move up the solution curve. Figure 6.3 illustrates how a product feature set that was originally designed for a specific kind of use case (customer need, situation, context of use) can evolve beyond enhanced features for that use case (incremental innovation) into the value of services that use the device as a delivery channel and enhance the value of the device. As more services are added, the product increases in value, whereas product-level feature enhancement may no longer provide enough value for the customer.

Once the level of service reaches a certain threshold, it can begin to unite different products into an ecosystem of devices (and additional services) that become a solution—a way to extend across a variety of connected needs. In many cases this new solution may completely change the way people do things and may make the original use case that the product was designed for no longer relevant.

The example here is Apple's iPod. The original use case was the need to transport MP3 files that a customer had created by "ripping" the CDs they had bought using computer software. It wasn't practical to bring the computer along everywhere you wanted to listen to the music. Of course, there was already a generation of MP3 players in the market when the iPod arrived. Not only did the iPod have different product-level features, but the iTunes software added value in that it was a library tool and a personal computer music player that synced a library with the iPod. With the addition of new devices (such as the Nano and Shuffle) and the ability to buy music directly through iTunes, Apple had extended the product-service into a rich ecosystem. This was further enhanced with new forms of content, beyond music, available through iTunes, the inclusion of different computer platforms, and eventually the addition of new devices (iPhone and iPad) and content (TV and movies). The original use case of buying CDs, ripping them to MP3s, and figuring out how to transport them is now considered a throwback. There is a generation of people who have never needed to buy a CD or rip files. (Apple also understands how this solution curve can be used to tie different product and service categories together and the level of customer engagement this can drive. We don't know if Apple ever thought of approaching its business in the same ways that we are structuring the concept of experience design, but the company provides a great example of the customer experience that can arise from such an approach.)

The important thing that product and service programs need to consider is how changes in use context affect decisions about how to develop the product or service.

Figure 6.3
The Solution Curve

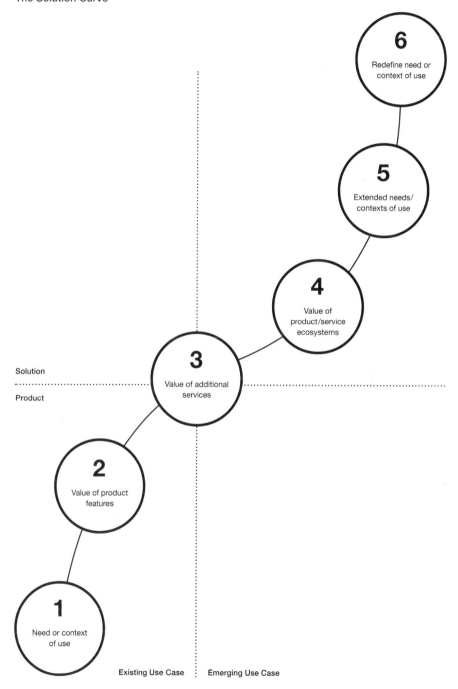

Figure 6.4 is a tool we use for thinking about use context for products and services. It is essentially a way to deconstruct a value proposition for a given customer (and need) in order to see what would really be going on in the customer's context before looking at how a product or service feature should be designed.

Once assumptions about the nature of a product or service have been made, it's often difficult to get the team that made the assumptions to consider new and relevant information in the right way. If the information contradicts what has already been committed to, it can easily be dismissed because it's outside of the product definition. Likewise, true consideration and change may be deemed be too costly and could put schedules at risk.

Figure 6.4 provides a framework for placing the user in the center and then looks at five components that help define the use context at that point in time. Additional components can be added, but these five are the basics—and it is better to add to these than to swap some of them out. To use this framework, begin by identifying who the "actor" (customer or user) is and which value proposition is going to be considered. This information can come directly from the needs and value framework.

The next step is to describe what's going on at each of the components based on the following description of what the components mean:

> Locations: List where the activity takes place, for example, home or office. Consider what changes when a location changes. How many locations are truly needed to complete a given task? For example, let's think about shopping. In the real world, we go to the store, we shop, we stand in the checkout line, we pay for the goods, we load the car, and we return home. When do we want to say we are really shopping? It's easy to compare this with online shopping and see how different the concept of location is between the two modes.
>
> Task(s): Identify the actions involved in satisfying the needs. These should be considered from the perspective of the customer's intent and goals, not from a product or service feature perspective.
>
> Devices: Identify the available products that are needed or are being used or that could be used by the customer.
>
> Data/information: Establish what data or information is needed to complete the task (data that is both consumed during the execution of the task and produced by the task execution) and how the data becomes available. This latter point should be considered in two ways: Where/who is the data coming from/going to, and what services are involved in the data exchange? If there are multiple streams, how do they integrate and share data and information?
>
> Emotion range: Document the normal range of emotions that are likely to arise in the larger context when customers carry out their tasks. Are they typically calm initially but stressed by the end? Are they bored and looking to be stimulated? Are they going to be anxious because the use context arises only in a stressful situation?

Figure 6.4
Value Proposition and Use Context Tool

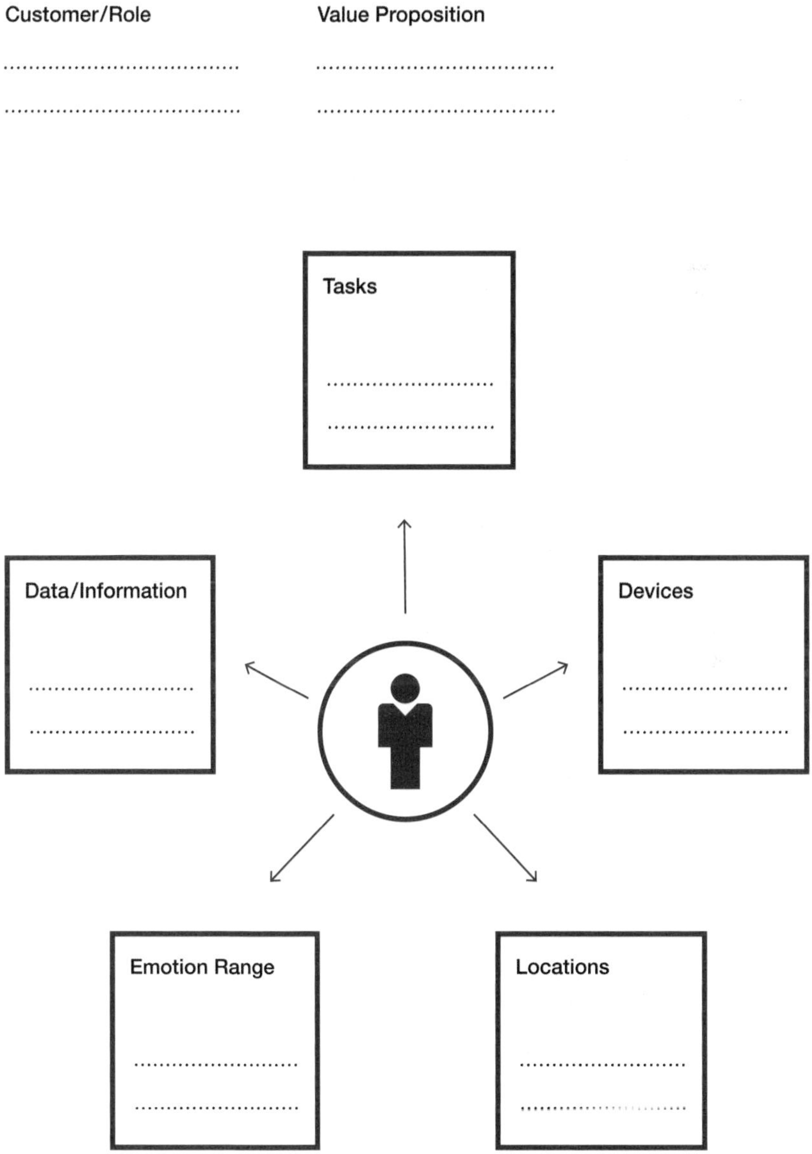

Customer/Role

Value Proposition

....

....

....

....

Tasks

....

....

Data/Information

....

....

Devices

....

....

Emotion Range

....

....

Locations

....

....

Other components that can be used in addition are time duration, user frequency, and collaboration with others. Of course, teams can add whatever components are useful for the product or service at hand.

Once an initial map has been produced that outlines a customer and a use context, it's time for a quick review. First, how many variations in locations and tasks exist? If you find that a given task can be fully completed only across two locations, this is good to know. If a given task can be done from multiple locations, this is also good to know.

Next, examine the location-task-device combinations. Are all locations and tasks served equally by the same device, or are other devices needed or desirable? If it's the same kind of device at different locations, is the actual device being used in both places, or are there two unique devices?

Last, look at the data and information to understand what data are needed, where the data will come from, what data might be produced, and what needs to happen to close the loop on the task. There are a few obvious things to look for, such as connectivity. Will a device that is a primary component of completing a task be able to get information or data the customer needs? How is the information or data being used, and how much work does the customer need to do to transfer information from one source into another (where the customer is getting the most value) with regard to the task and intent? Looking at information or data can also help determine what other customers or value propositions are connected, either through the completion of the task or a connection that exists upstream or downstream. A last point that is often ignored is what information or data can help the business providing the product or service understand and measure what is happening during the use of the product or service and what future needs can be met as a result.

If you're finding that there are really too many interdependencies to use a single map for a given customer scenario, then it's a simple task of create another and separate the information between the two. This allows you to explore the unique interdependencies that arise from specific combinations of task-location-device-data-emotion. You want to look for a few things when you do this. Does a really important customer come along with a lot of very complex issues to solve for, or does a task that is tied to a very important need become something that is very complex and actually very hard to solve for? Trying to solve for the more complex issue may compromise the quality of the solution being developed for the more basic value proposition.

All of this work also allows you to take one more step: mapping the use context to a service and device ecosystem—which is useful in making sure the product or service can deliver true value to a customer. In addition, this step highlights opportunities that may not have initially been considered. Through mapping, you can understand how the solution will work best for delivering value and identify future devices and services that could extend value for the customer.

Figure 6.5 is a device ecosystem framework. The purpose of this framework is to ensure that you have a good sense of what role each device in an ecosystem needs to play. Are the devices all mirror images of functionality and value, or are some more important than others? Although it's natural to think that they can and should be mirror images, the natural limitations of the devices or the way that customers tend to use them may suggest that they are not all equal. You'll also need to consider what services are available; for instance, although a home computer and a work computer may be exactly the same, the information made available to each may be different. The goal is to understand, before relying on or designing for a device, what the

Figure 6.5
Device Ecosystem Framework

Device Type		A	B	C	D
Device Specific	General Use Patterns				
	General Use Constraints				
Product/ Service Specific	Location of use				
	Value Propositions				
	Features				
	Interdependencies and Constraints				
	Use-contexts in which it is primary				
	Use-contexts in which it is secondary				
	Overall Importance				

UNIVERSITY OF WINCHESTER
LIBRARY

purpose is and what kinds of interdependencies are likely to arise. The added benefit is that you may also uncover gaps where no one has developed a particular service or device feature that could become a future milestone for your product or service. It might tie in to another product or service you provide that hadn't been associated with the use context. Perhaps there's a business model for data services that no one has stumbled upon, because it will come about only if a particular kind of solution or ecosystem gets adopted.

This process helps the team move from having a good sense of why a customer would find a product or service valuable (derived from the needs and value framework) to beginning to think about the variables in the actual experience of needs and need fulfillment that are likely to happen, regardless of what features are eventually decided on.

Following are a few points that are important to consider when doing this exercise:

- How reliant is the value of the product, service, or solution upon devices that aren't currently being addressed in the thinking?

- For devices that are currently addressed, how much control will you have over what kind of experience that can be delivered on the device (for example, how much does a device's operating system, form-factor, or content loading process dictate what is possible from an experience standpoint)?

- How many variations of this second point exist across similar devices provided by different manufacturers?

- How will you manage updates, version changes, and customer support across all of these variations?

In a nutshell, you need to consider what other devices customers are likely to use. This will help you understand what's possible to deliver (from both a value and experience perspective) and what's likely to be the best use of these devices given the customer expectations and the realities of what can be supported.

The goal is to highlight and understand the constraints that may affect design decisions in order to make sure that a product doesn't wind up having a proliferation of versions to meet a variety of use contexts. These can become difficult for the business to manage and can create poor experiences and big headaches for customers. This framework provides another opportunity to use the Brand, both through the Brand value pillars and attribute mapping framework, to influence how the experience and value can be differentiated and how managing some of the constraints are likely to affect the final experience a customer has with the product, service, or solution.

All of this can happen before final decisions have been made, and the process can be carried out iteratively, bringing in different teams. Although this may seem like we are pointing out the obvious, it's surprising how often business has gone far down the path in committing resources, time, and money only to find that they failed to account for some basic issues that will compromise customer value. The worst time to realize this is as you're finalizing messaging for a new product launch. Suddenly, you begin to realize that what you thought would be a compelling value proposition is actually very, very different and available only to a minority of the market and only in rare instances.

One other point we should make clear: Solutions and ecosystems are not limited to devices and the value propositions directly tied to technology. For example, consider the modern banking industry; banks are increasingly trying to position themselves as solutions providers for financial services to consumers. With the advent of ATMs and then online banking, the role of human-based interactions has shifted from an in-bank experience with tellers and managers to a series of screen-based interactions and call center support operators. Yet most banks still have a physical presence, and often, key transactions can happen only in person. This is a good representation of a service ecosystem that leverages multiple delivery channels.

What's interesting about the banking example are the opportunities that have not yet been fully explored to unite the experience across all the channels in order to create more value for the customer. For instance, a customer's history may be available to a bank manager who can see what issues may have arisen in an account and how they were addressed, but rarely does the support operator have a good sense of the relationship between the customer and the local bank manager. It raises the question of why banks have not made this connection. For instance, customer support could be provided with data that lets them ensure that a local, in-person interaction is available, perhaps even scheduling appointments for the customer. This would alleviate the breakdown that happens when the only effective way of fixing the customer's issue is in-person at the bank, but the customer doesn't realize this until after the bank has closed, leaving him or her with no alternative but to seek a remote customer support person.

We believe that the framework approach we suggest would help identify these kinds of opportunities that not only create value but also differentiate services. Experience design suggests that in addition to looking at how Brand informs value in a differentiated way, businesses should make sure they have the right breadth of information to fully understand the context in which the product or service will exist. Understanding the real nature of what a customer needs and is able to do with the product or service allows teams to think about how all the components involved in a solution work together, and prevents the team from jumping to conclusions or making assumptions that will leave gaps or create issues for the customer. The goal is to identify and iron out problems and avoid issues that lead to bad customer experiences before they actually become part of the product or service definition. If this goal isn't met, it can be impossible to "design" problems away.

Part 2
Extending Product and Service Thinking into Life Cycles

Anytime a customer buys a product or signs up for a service, there's a good chance that he or she has gone through one or more cognitive/emotional states as they navigate the customer journey with a given business. Although a full explanation of these stages is covered in the next chapter, we do want to introduce the concept here because of its importance for thinking about product and service experiences.

Generally, people don't spend money without a reason. The reasons we give ourselves for spending may be extremely well founded or nearly preposterous, but in general we are able to convince ourselves that we have some kind of need and what we are spending money on will in some way meet that need. This suggests two things: We have become aware of the option that we are about to spend money on, and we have, to some extent, considered how likely it is that we will be satisfied with our purchase.

Why is this important? Because what's happening is that a customer has likely begun to frame his or her expectation before actually taking ownership or beginning a service relationship. The gap between what they expect and what they get is something that should be of concern to the business (because we assume that any business that's looking to grow relationships with customers would agree that satisfaction with the relationship is crucial). Business can reduce this gap in many ways, including by giving people access to try products before buying, such as through free introductory service trials. These are useful and good practices, especially when the approach to defining, designing, and developing the product or service has taken into account a user life cycle.

A user life cycle represents the different stages involved in using a product or service. We differentiate these from a customer life cycle, but really they can be considered as a subset. The important thing to recognize is that a user's frame of reference will shift as the person uses a product or service. This is both an opportunity and a challenge for business and design. (And we should point out that there is a strong overlap with the field of human factors and processes such as user-centered design. The main difference is that we want to focus on areas that pertain to the experience of specific value and not just best practices for design methodology.)

Let's start with the challenge. When a customer first encounters a product or service there are two things he or she is likely to be thinking about: What is my expectation, and what is the mental model of what I am about to do? By *mental model* we mean what does the customer think he or she is getting into, and how familiar is the person with this context (what it's about, what to expect, how to do things)?

There are several ways that things go wrong as a result of shortcomings of business and design planning and execution. It's natural to want to create demand for a product or service and, in doing so, talk about all the wonderful things it does. The benefits of use are often chosen as the most effective way of communicating with prospective customers. Many times this is done without a strong reference to how the product or service actually works. The disconnect that arises is when a customer begins to use the product or service and has no way of understanding how to use it or what to do to get the value desired, which was the reason that the person decided to spend money. This can happen with products and services that people are familiar with but which have undergone some level of "innovation." The example we love is the hybrid car. A few of our executives had rented a car for a trip. They got in the car as usual but were unable to operate it—although they had been driving for decades, they had never driven this particular hybrid. They actually had to search the Internet to find out how to release the parking brake and engage the transmission.

Users' mental models are also tied to their expectations of value. We would draw a slight conceptual distinction between the two, because people may have a preexisting mental model that is fairly accurate but may still need help following a path to get the expected value. The other difference is that a mental model for a specific product or service does not need to change over time, whereas it might be a good idea to introduce new value paths over time to make sure users can still get value from a product or service. Value paths can be intrinsic or extrinsic. In many cases the product or service road map is the plan for increasing intrinsic value. However, some products are so complex that it's a good idea to think about how to make these value paths more explicit to users.

Often, the marketing and promotion of a product or service does not do a good job of conveying the right mental model, and frequently they do not have a great opportunity for presenting value paths, especially if they are of short duration and focused on imprinting some level of positive emotion. It is also frequently the case with complex products that those creating the marketing and messaging may not be familiar enough with the value paths to be able to use them in any meaningful way.

Another common and perhaps bigger problem is that in defining, designing, and developing the product or service, there have been too many assumptions about the user's familiarity with the mental model needed and their ability to find and follow value paths.

The previous frameworks we presented in this chapter were largely aimed at helping business and design ensure that adequate value exists in every product and service. This one, although fairly basic, is intended to ensure that the customer can actually get to the value when using the product or service and, perhaps more important, that there is an opportunity for the business to maintain and increase the customer's perception of value over time.

It's easy to conceive of how a product or service should work when you're fairly familiar with the basic concept of what it's supposed to do. On the other hand, it's difficult to think about what the same product or service will be like to someone who is completely unfamiliar with it. However, being accommodating for the first-time user can also be a problem for experienced users who may want better efficiency or control. Conventions that help people orient and learn may become a nuisance later on. There is no perfect way to anticipate every situation, but it's worth thinking about how things will vary between first-time use and final use for your most important customers.

The framework shown in Figure 6.6 can help you take the needs and value propositions framework and determine what would be important to consider for the customers who are most important for the successful adoption of your product or service. Anticipate what would be required for mainstream adoption and what might make the first generation of customers leave because it no longer meets their needs. The process should begin with the identification of the customer and primary value proposition. The answers to the questions become design criteria against which proposed solutions can be evaluated. It should be clear that the more detail involved in answering the questions, the more effective the criteria can be at guiding a better outcome.

Figure 6.6
Mental Model and Value Path Framework

Customer	Primary Value Propositions	Question to Ask	Details to Answer
		What mental model might they have?	▪ Do they have previous expectations? ▪ Will they expect certain kinds of features? ▪ Will it be a completely alien experience, for which they have no idea what to expect?
		What mental model do I want them to have?	▪ Do you want to position the product or service in a specific way? ▪ Is there a mental model that would make learning to use the product or service easier? ▪ Do future features, or areas of value, rely on customers understanding existing features that are based on new concepts or unfamiliar processes?
		How do we help them form the right mental model?	▪ How does the product or service experience need to be organized to support the right mental model? ▪ What other ways/touch points in the customer experience should be used to help support the right mental model? ▪ When should the process of developing a new model start? (Advertising? Point of sale? First Use?)
		What are the key value paths that allow them to quickly get to the value they expect?	▪ Will they know how to quickly access and use the features that deliver the expected value propositions?
		What are the potential pitfalls and problems?	▪ Will approaches to supporting first-time users become a problem for ongoing use?
		When are they likely to need more value and what will that be?	▪ At what point will it be logical to introduce or suggest new features? ▪ How will they discover them? ▪ Will future releases integrate with the existing experience? ▪ What patterns or behaviors should be established to make future features easier to use or more likely to be perceived as valuable?
		When is the customer likely to move beyond the value of this product and service and what will you provide?	▪ What would lead a customer to need more than the product or service they are currently using? ▪ What would the cues be and how would the product or service respond? ▪ How would you make them aware of new products or services? ▪ Where and when would this take place?

Other Frameworks

The other aspect of time and life cycle that can be useful to consider involves looking across potential stages of use (and need) of a specific touch point with which customers will come in contact. There are many customer touch points that are somewhat taken for granted. They play a specific functional role but aren't considered as significant for the customer experience. In some cases these are missed opportunities to provide value. It's also worth considering other aspects of use that might affect costs.

Figure 6.7 applies this kind of thinking to packaging. Packaging has many functional uses over the course of its lifetime, in addition to being part of the customer experience. Choices that affect one end of the life cycle may also have an impact on other areas.

The important takeaway is that thinking upstream and downstream from a specific opportunity helps business and design understand how a product or service will exist in the real world. It's easy to assume that all the requirements can be identified simply by thinking through the business model, the customer, and the needs being targeted. It's better to understand the broader implication of time and how this changes the context—before defining requirements or beginning development. This will also help put the team in the right frame of mind for using the customer journey framework as a tool for experience design, which we describe in Chapter 7.

Figure 6.7
A Version of a Packaging Life Cycle

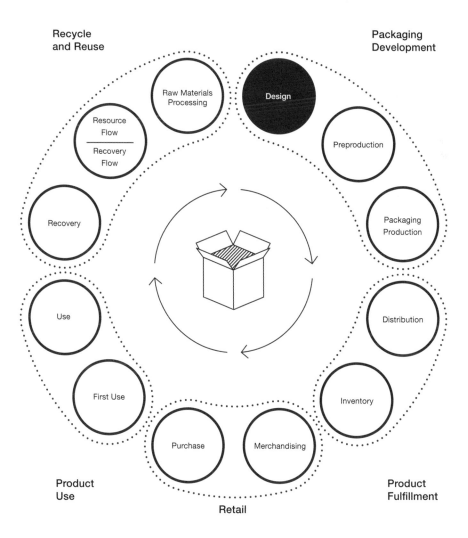

Recycle
and Reuse

Packaging
Development

Raw Materials
Processing

Design

Resource
Flow
———
Recovery
Flow

Preproduction

Recovery

Packaging
Production

Use

Distribution

First Use

Inventory

Purchase

Merchandising

Product
Use

Product
Fulfillment

Retail

Part 3
Trend and Implication Framework

The final framework is a tool for exploring new opportunities and helping identify areas in which to pursue sustaining and down-market innovations. It can also be used to organize and develop ideas that seem like they could be disruptive innovations.

As we pointed out in Chapter 3, businesses are faced with a need for constant evolution—relentless innovation—because they need to constantly react to changes in the larger business and technology environment. Although not every change requires a dramatic response and not every opportunity will represent a substantial innovation in value, it's useful to have mechanisms through which to filter change and see what could be done. From there, you can determine what to follow up with and for what reason.

Figure 6.8 shows the trend and implication framework. To use this framework, begin by identifying a trend that may be noteworthy for your business. This can include macro-level changes in society or regulation, emerging technology, or new kinds of products or services. What's important here is providing some kind of definition and description of the trend that will allow you to begin to provide information in one or more of the following areas:

> Examples: Products or services that represent the trend

> Emerging needs and behaviors: What people are doing as a result of having access to these new products or services or as a result of the broader change that defines and describes the change

> Touch points: The actual new products and services or other things people are likely to encounter as a result of changes in activities, tasks, or a different way of using of existing products and services

Generate ideas and consider other implications for needs and opportunities that could be met through existing products and services or through experiences that the business could provide to customers. Because these will often be fairly forward-looking ideas or because emerging needs and opportunities may not have been researched and validated, the next step is to filter the ideas generated to determine how these ideas might support business goals. This can help guide both research and prioritization of the importance in pursuing specific ideas.

Figure 6.8
Trend and Implication Framework

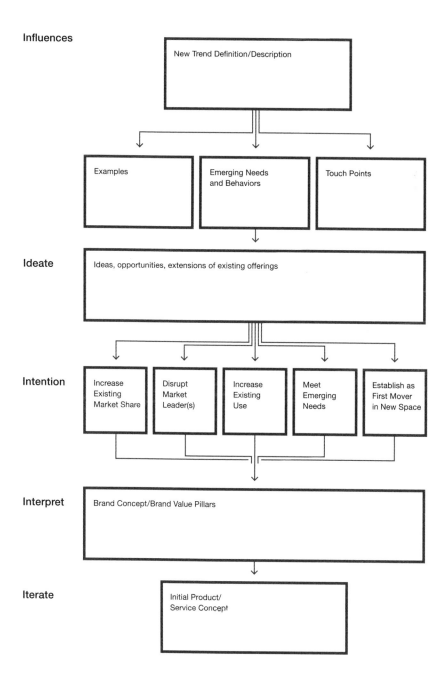

Influences

New Trend Definition/Description

Examples

Emerging Needs
and Behaviors

Touch Points

Ideate

Ideas, opportunities, extensions of existing offerings

Intention

Increase
Existing
Market Share

Disrupt
Market
Leader(s)

Increase
Existing
Use

Meet
Emerging
Needs

Establish as
First Mover
in New Space

Interpret

Brand Concept/Brand Value Pillars

Iterate

Initial Product/
Service Concept

The categories used for intention can be modified, but the basics include the following five items:

> Increase market share: Specifically grow the existing customer share by providing more value or a differentiated form of value that the competition cannot match.

> Disrupt market leader(s): Provide a level of value at a price point that undercuts a competitor or makes the need that a competitor serves irrelevant.

> Increase existing use: Provide a new feature or add value for an existing product or service that increases usage, especially for services that produce revenue based on use.

> Meet emerging needs: Based on existing use patterns and need fulfillment, provide the next logical value.

> Establish as first mover in new space: Introduce a new product, service, or feature to reinforce aspects of the Brand concept or to position the Brand's understanding of where new value is likely to be sought by customers.

This is a useful step to go through because an initial idea might have a range of different possibilities, which will have different levels of risk and cost associated with how they are approached. By assessing which directions are most useful to the business, the appropriate scope and level of investment can be determined. This will also allow for a conversation about what level of effort makes sense based on a cost/benefit analysis.

After this, ideas can be interpreted through the Brand concept and Brand value pillars to better contextualize how an idea would complement the existing Brand offering and explore how it might be influenced by or connected to the broader customer experience. Following this, we suggest using some or all of the previous frameworks in this section to further iterate and develop the idea.

Experience design is based on the assumptions that value is important and that the more information is considered and the broader the context, the more value can be delivered in ways that meet a full life cycle of customer needs. It's easy to dismiss the value of information and rush to market with ideas, especially if they are new. The problem is that there is a limit to customers' tolerance for having their expectations unmet by a Brand and there are limits to how much money people have to spend.

7

Customer Journey Framework

So far we have been discussing experience design from some relatively narrow and internally focused perspectives: Brand and products/services. In this chapter we will delve more deeply into how these perspectives tie in to the ways in which customers experience value.

Nearly every large company we've worked with has had some form of a customer journey that they use to help teams understand how the marketing and sales process works. It's also a way to focus on the efforts that are most likely to pull prospects into the "funnel" before converting them into customers and ringing the sales bell. Companies that understand the importance of customer experience will often extend their customer journey to include stages that address what happens after the sale, largely with an eye toward how to keep in contact with a customer (and keep the customer primed for future purchases).

Our approach to experience design suggests taking the concept of a customer journey and extending its uses beyond the marketing, sales, and relationship management functions. It suggests using it as a way to understand what the Brand is really doing in the world from the perspective of how the Brand's efforts are experienced and interpreted by people who aren't immersed in the planning and execution of these efforts. One of the benefits of this approach is that it forces people to think in context of time (time as it relates to the continuity of experience) and perceptions that a customer has with the Brand. It gives you a chance to see what changes in the customer's understanding of the products and services a Brand offers over time. It highlights where the business focus typically ends as compared with the customer's focus. It may even help show the business things that might be going on that the company was not aware of. As an organization begins to train itself to think this way, it can begin to ask three questions: Are we creating value for our customers? Are we making them more likely to stay engaged with us? Are we differentiating our Brand and making it stronger? The company should be able to answer these with both actual knowledge and focused intent.

One of the interesting things we've seen with our clients is a shift in thinking that begins to provide tactical projects with long-term goals by providing a context that helps teams see how a small effort is part of something bigger. They can see how incremental steps shape the overall customer experience and how actions in one stage of the customer experience can influence later stages—both positively and negatively. It also helps decision makers realize and plan how strategic business goals might better be tackled through a portfolio of smaller initiatives that are actually less risky and help bring change about in a more controlled and efficient manner. Even companies that recognize that they need to change direction pretty quickly get mired down because so many activities have interdependencies with one another and change in one area can only be fully realized by changing all areas. The inertia created when change is against the particular business interests or functional efficiency of a key constituency can lead to a logjam that may result in efforts being abandoned. Or the acceptance that "we are now too big to change" is followed by the resignation to a slow stagnation.

We believe that much of the success in any endeavor comes through successful management of efforts over time with a clarity of objectives, an understanding of the benefits of actions, and a clear plan for where and when efforts can be most useful.

The customer journey framework plays a key role in experience design because it's a mechanism for prompting these conversations in a nonthreatening way—by talking about value to the customer as value to the business.

Framework Background

The customer journey we suggest using for experience design differs from others we have seen in several ways. There is room for interpretation and adaptation, but we suggest that anyone who uses a framework like this for experience design should be aware of how his or her approach integrates the principles of experience design with some of the basic components of the thinking.

Four observations have had a strong influence on our approach to a customer journey framework, and we think they are helpful to understand before we explain how this framework can be used. The first observation is that to be an effective tool, the framework must be relevant for business and design. We believe that the fundamental aspect of business intent and meaning for a Brand arising from real-world customer experience is the foundation on which this framework (and our thinking on experience design, in general) rests. If we agree that business needs to constantly react and plan for creating and delivering value in a changing environment, then this approach to experience design would help ensure that the strategy, expression, and general categories of value are well understood and available to teams who need to define, design, develop, and deliver value to customers. We believe that it's easier to manage a portfolio of related efforts (across the customer experience) than it is to make huge individual bets.

Figure 7.1 is a schematic representation of how these efforts are organized and can change over time. All of these efforts eventually play out in the customer journey. The key is to consider where the customer is in his or her journey and what he or she finds valuable. E-mailing existing customers with promotions for new releases may not rank high on their value meter, especially if they already have existing needs you aren't aware of connected with using your existing products or services. When thinking about creating experiences that engage around value, it's always good to get outside of the transaction-centric view that can be too easy for businesses to use as a default.

Figure 7.1
Using a Portfolio of Customer Experience Initiatives
to Support the Customer Journey

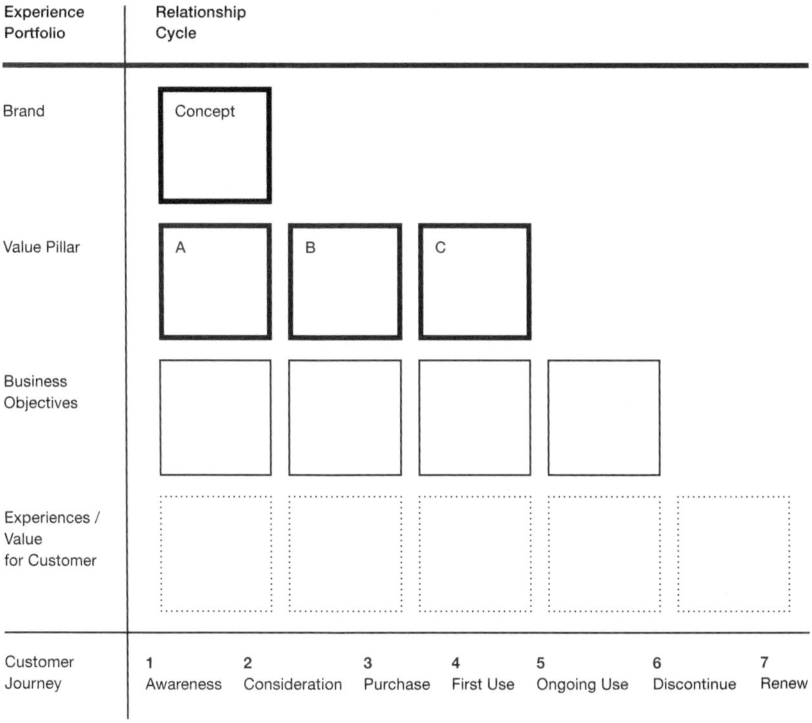

Experience Portfolio	Relationship Cycle						
Brand	Concept						
Value Pillar	A	B	C				
Business Objectives							
Experiences / Value for Customer							
Customer Journey	1 Awareness	2 Consideration	3 Purchase	4 First Use	5 Ongoing Use	6 Discontinue	7 Renew

The second observation that has influenced the development of our framework is that customers may have a very different perspective on what's important than what business would like or expect. In Chapter 4 we introduced a formula for perceived value and referenced it again as we outlined the foundational concepts of our approach to experience design.

We will bring it back one more time here:

$$\text{Perceived Value} = \frac{\left(\begin{array}{c}\text{What has been done or}\\\text{provided by a business}\end{array}\right) - \left[\left(\begin{array}{c}\text{Customer}\\\text{needs}\end{array}\right) \times \left(\begin{array}{c}\text{Customer}\\\text{expectations}\end{array}\right)\right]}{\text{Customer context}}$$

What we want business and design to think about when considering the customer is where the customer's head is at any given stage of a customer journey. What is the customer coming to the table with, and what will an experience need to do to be perceived as being valuable and positive? Too many customer journey maps that we have seen simply define the stage of the relationship with the business, not with what is important from the customer's point of view. We don't propose that there is an off-the-shelf framework that can tell you what a person is thinking or what an individual's priorities may be, but we do believe that if your framework suggests it's important information to consider, you are more likely to ask the question, What does my customer really need at this point; what would really make a difference?

Many customer journey maps that are used with quality of experience in mind place an emphasis on touch points and how they are used at different stages of the journey. Just as we believe that decisions about how to deliver value should not come before answers to why something will be of value, we believe that which touch points are used and how they are used should be driven by serving the customer, not by what's the standard practice for business to do at a specific stage of the journey. Another reason this view is useful is that it helps free the thinking to incorporate new touch points or use existing ones in innovative ways. Otherwise, it's too easy to limit thinking to conventional approaches.

Figure 7.2 schematically shows the hierarchy of customer needs elements that we suggest using as a starting point. These can be modified based on the nature of the customer, the Brand and the products or services it offers, and the stage of the journey. The basic point is to realize that a customer has a rational thought process and an emotional thought process. These processes shape the pragmatic needs, related to any stage of the journey, that help the customer make forward progress through the journey. We believe that experience design requires business and design to carefully consider all these needs before deciding which touch points to use and how to use them.

Figure 7.2
Customer Needs

The customer's goal for any given stage
of their journey with a business is their
combined needs, thought processes, influences,
and intended actions

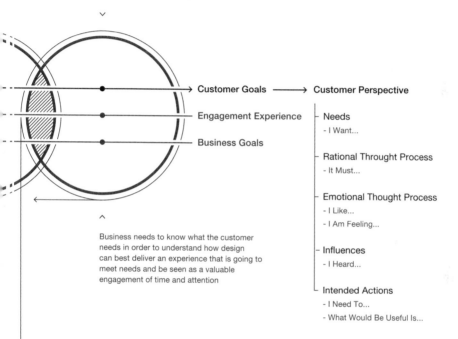

Customer Goals ⟶ Customer Perspective

Engagement Experience ├ Needs
  - I Want...

Business Goals └ Rational Throught Process
  - It Must...

├ Emotional Thought Process
  - I Like...
  - I Am Feeling...

Business needs to know what the customer
needs in order to understand how design
can best deliver an experience that is going to
meet needs and be seen as a valuable
engagement of time and attention

├ Influences
  - I Heard...

└ Intended Actions
  - I Need To...
  - What Would Be Useful Is...

#
Stage of the Journey

The third observation is that looking at things as stages in a journey is both necessary and wrong. It's wrong because not all people go through the same stages in the same ways, and for prospects that become customers, the journey may be much more of a cycle than a journey. The challenge is that cycles can be hard to dissect and look at in ways that allow for specific insights and opportunity identification—they often lack a mutually agreed-upon reference point. We choose to use a linear representation simply because of the ease of use it represents, not because the journey has a universal beginning and end point.

Connected to this thought is the perspective that even looking at stage boundaries too concretely is a disservice. As we said, not everyone goes through the stages in the same way, nor should they. The goal is for people to progress from being prospective customers, to being actual customers, to being satisfied and engaged customers. We use the idea that stages can have a degree of overlap to capture the lack of true delineation between stages and, more important, to remind business and design thinkers that the goal is not merely to serve needs and deliver value within the current stage but to think about how this helps move customers from one stage to the next. This also reinforces the idea that thinking about what's going on in the customer's head is important, because understanding possible stage-entry barriers is a good way to understand how to improve the transition. It is less effective to look at it as if each stage has a hard boundary and then doing everything to fulfill the intraboundary needs.

Figure 7.3 shows how we represent this overlap between stages of the customer journey. We think that in defining experiences for the customer journey, creating value for customers that addresses the intersection of stages and helps a customer move forward creates higher degrees of engagement and makes transitions more natural.

Figure 7.3
Targeting the Overlap Between Stages of the Customer Journey
to Drive Engagement and Help Transition Customer

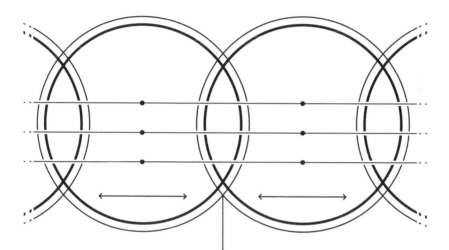

Information and interactions
designed to support customer goals in
the current stage of the customer journey

Information and interactions
designed to support customer goals in
the current stage of the customer journey

Information and interactions
designed to support customer goals
in multiple stages, with the aim of
moving the customer forward to the
next stage

The last observation that has influenced our approach to the customer journey was recognizing the overlap between what we were trying to do with the framework and the concept of service blueprinting (a part of the practice of many service design methodologies). The premise of the service blueprint is that there may be multiple levels of effort that need to occur to deliver value at a specific stage through specific touch points. This may not be adequately represented through a description of the touch point, and it may require a bit of planning, definition, and design to fully identify all of the necessary components and how they need to work together.

A service design blueprint typically shows activities that are done on behalf of, in front of, or with the customer. It also shows additional activities that may need to take place either in parallel or immediately before or after activities that a customer experiences. It also shows which touch points are used in the experience, which helps business and design planners determine whether there are more effective ways to use existing touch points, whether some are superfluous, or whether there is an obvious need for a touch point that doesn't exist at that stage. It also shows that there may be a variety of parties involved, both with the customer and behind the scenes. This allows planners to understand how all the components of an experience are accounted for and choreographed, and it ensures that ownership and responsibility are clearly assigned and accepted.

Figure 7.4 is a schematic of how we refer to the different touch points and roles that are part of delivering an experience. When looking at the entire customer journey, we typically do not represent the behind-the-scenes activities, because this will vary based on the business and the experience. We have started using data as a component, because this has implications regarding who is needed or involved in activities and who is frequently overlooked.

Figure 7.4
Touch Points and Roles for Stages of the Customer Journey

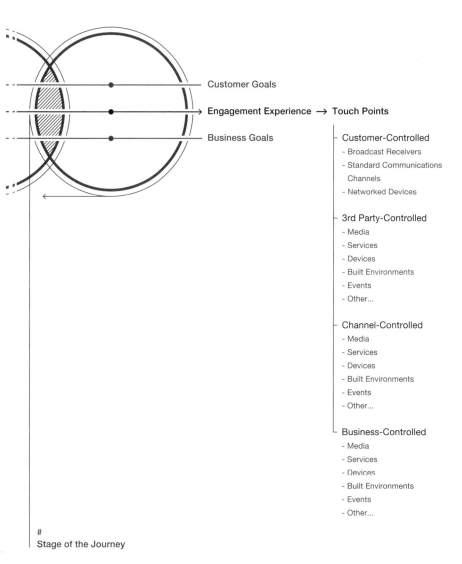

Customer Goals

Engagement Experience → Touch Points

Business Goals

⊢ Customer-Controlled
- Broadcast Receivers
- Standard Communications
  Channels
- Networked Devices

⊢ 3rd Party-Controlled
- Media
- Services
- Devices
- Built Environments
- Events
- Other...

⊢ Channel-Controlled
- Media
- Services
- Devices
- Built Environments
- Events
- Other...

⊢ Business-Controlled
- Media
- Services
- Devices
- Built Environments
- Events
- Other...

\#
Stage of the Journey

The Customer Journey Framework

Over the years we have used many variations of this framework, but the basic model has not changed substantially. Figure 7.5 shows the overall framework. The number of stages will depend on the nature of the product or service, the customer's purchase process, and how the product or service will be used. The stages we normally use will be described, and you can use this approach as an outline for developing or adding stages to a customized version for a specific business.

Figure 7.5
A Prototypical Customer Journey Framework

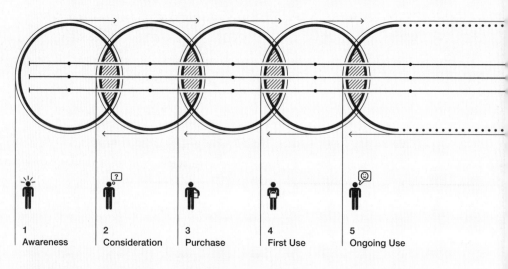

1 Awareness	2 Consideration	3 Purchase	4 First Use	5 Ongoing Use
A customer becomes aware of a particular business, Brand, or product/service; he/she begins to realize that he/she has a need.	The process of formalizing needs and weighing alternatives. This includes acting on needs but can also include the decision not to do anything.	The decision to buy a product or service: the final stage of the customer acting on his/her needs; usually covers the transaction process up until first use.	This is the customer's first unaided use of the product or service (sometimes called the out-of-box experience), where his/her expectations meet reality.	Regular ongoing use and: Emergence of new needs (through discovering features or finding gaps in value provided) and formalization of these needs into actions Problems that prevent realization of expected value (either through defects or lack of knowledge on how to use the product or service) Sharing his/her experiences with other people through actions or words (either directly or indirectly).

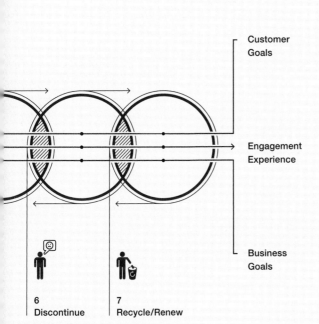

Customer
Goals

Customer Perspective
Needs
Rational Thought Process
Emotional Thought Process
Influences
Intended Actions

Engagement
Experience

Touch points
Customer-Controlled
3rd Party-Controlled
Channel-Controlled
Business-Controlled

Business
Goals

Business Perspective
Partners/Channels
IT Systems of Engagement
Marketing/Sales
Support/CRM
Finance/Operations

6
Discontinue

The end of product
or service use,
because of
obsolescence,
business failure,
lack of interest
or perceived value
by customer, or
changes in his/her
circumstances.

7
Recycle/Renew

The process
of disposing of
a product and
the re-engaging
with a service,
perhaps through
a new product.

1
Awareness

In general, this stage—awareness—covers two things: when the customer becomes aware of a particular business/Brand and when the customer starts to realize that he or she has a need for it. Often, customer journeys focus on the former, but we suggest that a sound approach to experience design should also consider the latter. Understanding when needs begin to emerge can allow for an earlier and stronger imprinting on the customer.

Some of the questions that should be considered when looking at this stage follow:

Brand-Centric
- When does the customer first become aware of the Brand, the products, and the services being offered?
- How does the customer begin to build an understanding of why these might be relevant to him or her?
- What products and services are available?
- How are they relevant to the customer?
- Does the customer have an understanding of what the Brand is and what the Brand stands for?

Need-Centric
- How do the needs that a product or service serves generally emerge within a customer's mind?
- What are the prompts that tend to make a customer aware of a need, and what are the behavioral cues of a customer who has identified a need?
- Are there certain life-stage events or circumstances in which creating awareness of products and services can trigger the recognition of need?
- Are there related needs that become effective on-ramps to setting the stage for future needs?

2
Consideration

The consideration stage deals with the process of formalizing needs and weighing alternatives. This includes acting on needs but can also include the decision not to do anything. The circumstances and psychology of the individual begin to have a big influence at this stage. Some people may be impulsive and quick to act; others may need a long time to build a logical rationale to support their decision.

We like to think of two sides of mind being served here. The first is considering the information and facts. The other is more emotional, and we often describe the end goal for this as the customers seeing themselves as (happy) product owners or service users. (There is a point at which they need to convince and reassure themselves to move forward.) It may be difficult to tease these two mind-sets apart, but it's useful to realize that what may seem like a rational approach may have a more emotional background process and vice versa.

Some of the questions that should be considered when looking at this stage follow:

- Has the customer formed opinions about the Brand?
- Has he or she obtained enough information about the products and services?
- Do the products and services meet his or her needs?
- Does he or she understand what the alternatives are?
- Has he or she begun to form an opinion about which provider will be the best choice?
- Has he or she reached the point of making a decision regarding which provider to use?
- Has he or she thought of themselves as a product owner/service user?
- Is he or she thinking about ownership and how the product or service will provide value?
- Has he or she accepted the financial implications?
- Does he or she need more information to help make decisions?
- Does he or she need a reason to make a choice (of which provider to use or whether to actually buy)?

3
Purchase

The purchase stage is when the customer is intending to act on his or her decision. Several things should be considered here, but the basic idea is to make the experience as easy, seamless, and confidence building as possible. Part of this means lowering barriers, but part of it also means making sure the customer will continue to have confidence in the decision made. When a decision is not based on a strong need or motivation, problems during the purchase process can lead to buyer's remorse and even the smallest snags during the next stage can lead to returns or cancellations.

Some of the questions that should be considered when looking at this stage follow:

- Does the customer know where to buy?
- Does the customer know how to buy?
- What information will be required in order to make the purchase?
- What is the transaction process, and what variables are involved?
- How long will it take?
- What has to happen between the transaction and receiving the product or accessing the service?
- How long will the gap between purchase and use be?
- What happens during that time?

4
First Use

This stage—first use—is one that is often underserved and can be the key to building a good customer relationship and favorable Brand beliefs. This is where the customer's expectation meets the reality of what the product or service actually does. We mentioned the "Oh shit!" moment earlier in the book; this is when that can happen. A goal of an experience design approach is to ensure this doesn't happen and the path to use and value is as short, smooth, and intuitive as possible. We often call this the out-of-box experience, and this is where the efforts of many different business functions can either integrate to create a wonderful experience or focus solely on individual goals, leaving the customer to figure out what to do.

Some of the questions that should be considered when looking at this stage follow:

- How likely is it that the customer will be able to get value from the product or service immediately?
- What is the out-of-box or setup and activation experience?
- How easy is it, and can the customer do it?
- Are there likely to be problems?
- What is the support process?
- What is the availability of support?
- Will support be able to handle all customer issues?
- What kind of issues would require the customer to return a product and what would the return process be in this situation?
- Assuming that the issue can be resolved, how long is it likely to take before the customer is using the product or service?
- If the customer decides he or she does not want the product or service at this point, is returning the product still an option, and how might this return process need to differ from other return processes?

5
Ongoing Use

The stage of ongoing use is the time during which the customer has day-to-day experiences with the product or service. While considering the overall customer journey, this is often seen as a single stage. Much of what happens here will be defined by the actual product or service and the use contexts and value propositions that go along with this definition (and the actual design and deployment). Depending on their experience, customers may positively or negatively influence other customers or prospects. Customers may also discover new and unexpected needs, leading to an awareness of options and the decision to act.

An experience design approach not only looks for ways to make the regular use one that provides easy perceived value but also anticipates future needs or begins to create usage patterns that help identify future needs as they emerge. This is especially important if product or service road maps and business goals rely on adoption of new features or service upgrades. In addition, seeing how one person's use can begin to drive greater awareness in others helps product managers use this stage to leverage overall business growth. This includes helping customers become evangelists and advocates, as well as using functional approaches that provide value to the customer but also connect new prospects to the product or service.

Some of the variations that we suggest considering during this stage follow:

General Product or Service Use
- How often is a customer likely to use a product or service?
- How much effort is needed from the initiation of use to realization of value for any use context?
- How does this time affect the customer's likelihood of using the product or service?
- What would make the customer more likely to use the product or service?
- Are there other circumstances that would have an impact on how much the product or service gets used?

Emergence of New Needs
- What are the likely new needs that will come about as a customer uses the product or service?
- Are these needs the result of the limitations of the value provided by the product or service, or the result of new use contexts that are made possible by the product or service?
- Do emerging needs change the customer's current perception of value regarding the existing product or service?

Formalization of New Needs

- How does the product or service meet or support the emerging needs?
- Is it clear how to access the features that meet these needs?
- What other information might be needed or useful to help the customer formalize his or her needs?
- How does the customer become aware of this information, and where does the customer access it?
- Does the product's or service's inability to meet these formalized needs change the relationship the customer has with the Brand?
- Is there a competitor positioned to meet these newly formalized needs?

Experiencing Problems or Issues

- What kinds of problems or issues is a customer likely to have, and are these related to usability or are they potential breakdowns of the product or problems with the service?
- How is the probability of these problems or issues arising tied to the length of time using the service?
- How will this relationship affect how the customer feels about a problem or issue occurring?
- How will a customer know whether a problem or issue is occurring or if he or she is just doing something wrong?

Solving Problems or Issues

- How will the customer know that a problem is solvable?
- How will the customer get support?
- What information will the customer need?
- What is the process, and how long is it likely to take?
- What is the probability that a problem will actually be solved?

Solution Evaluation
- Does the problem or issue appear to be fixed?
- How likely is it that it will reoccur?
- How long will the customer likely remain concerned that the problem might not have been solved?
- If the problem can't be solved, what are the options for the customer?
- How likely is it that the customer will be satisfied with these options?

Influencing Others
- How likely is it that other people will be influenced by the experiences a customer has with a given product or service?
- How likely is it that a customer will share his or her opinion?
- What would make it more likely that a customer will share a favorable opinion?
- What would make it more likely that a customer will share an unfavorable opinion?
- Where and why are opinions most likely to be shared?
- When and why are opinions most likely to carry weight?

6
Discontinue Use

Eventually people stop using products and services. This can be a result of a change in circumstances—life stage or finances—or it can be because of obsolescence, business failure, or lack of interest or perceived value.

When taking an experience design approach to Brand, experience, and value, this stage is both a good learning opportunity and a potential place to introduce new value or reinvigorate the relationship with the customer.

Some of the questions that should be considered when looking at this stage follow:

- Are the reasons for discontinuing use tied to the performance of the product or service?
- If the provider of the product or service could overcome any shortcomings in value, would the customer care?
- Could shortcomings be fixed or alleviated in future versions of the product or service?
- Are the reasons for discontinuing use tied directly to the product or service itself or related to new options available that provide enhanced value?
- Have the needs and use contexts that the product or service was designed for changed or gone away?
- What are the feelings that arise about the product or service and the Brand as a result of discontinuing use?
- How does discontinued use affect the relationship between the customer and the business?

7
Recycle / Renew

After a customer makes the decision to discontinue use of a product or service, there are often two needs that arise. One is disposing of the product. Depending on the nature of the product and the mind-set of the customer, this may require something more significant than simply throwing the product away. Some products (such as cars and appliances) are too big to simply throw out, and many products will not be accepted by municipal trash management services. There is also an altruistic aspect in that the product still may be of use to others. Through an experience design approach, providing ways to support the customer with his or her desire or need to recycle products will help maintain customer engagement.

With services, the decision to discontinue use or terminate may be temporary, or changes in the value proposition may encourage renewed usage. With products, a new version of the product may be introduced that makes the existing option less desirable, or less effective when compared to the new alternative. Either of these situations can lead to a second need—renewing or restarting use of a product or service. In the case of services, having a good understanding of why a service was discontinued can lead to opening the door to future service usage, especially if the issue is temporary and there would be value for the customer in being able to pick up where he or she left off in the near future.

Some of the questions that should be considered when looking at this stage follow:

- What is the customer likely to do with a product after discontinuing use?
- Is disposing of the product a problem? If so, how can value be created through helping the customer solve this problem?
- Is there a secondary market for the product or its components?
- Does the customer's perception of the Brand benefit from helping the customer recycle the product?
- Does the customer's perception of the Brand benefit from helping others get access to discarded products that are still usable?
- Is there value in providing future access to account information or data that is used for a service?
- Is there value in having a service to help plan for termination, reinstallation, or reactivation at a future point in time?

Using the Customer Journey Framework

We believe that the customer journey framework is a great multipurpose tool for experience design. We like to use it as one lens to consider almost any problem, even if the actual work involved does not require directly applying it. If nothing else, it helps bring a multidimensional mind-set to the framing and evaluation of a problem and almost always allows for a novel insight.

There are three specific approaches to using this framework that support how our experience design methodologies can create a more effective way for business and design to work together. Each is based on applying the principles and basic components of experience design and uses the framework as a tool for visualizing, communicating, evaluating, or generating ideas and concepts. What we find most useful about the framework is that it makes it very easy to see how and where efforts can help improve the customer experience or deliver more value; it also helps conversations move out of the subjective interpretation stage or stops them from being filtered through a functional or departmental screen.

Sharing Views and Efforts

We strongly believe that the right conversations are not always being had regarding how business and design should be working and what is really important: value for customers and engagement that leads to higher lifetime value of customers. Versions of this conversation do take place, but often decisions are made or assumptions are reached that are not well informed or that could be more effective with minimal additional effort.

We believe that a main reason for this is the lack of vocabulary and forum for these discussions. It's very easy to brush aside concerns as being irrelevant when they are outside of one's functional domain. It's also difficult to understand why something should be done if the results aren't going to immediately benefit how one's success is measured.

The customer journey framework can be used simply to ask questions about how actions in one area will be affected by actions in other areas and what planners intend or would like to see as next steps for the actions they want to set in motion. With nothing to reference, these conversations can be difficult.

Using the framework as a graphic tool for asking these kinds of questions helps people see the potential diversity of things that might need to be addressed. It can help remove the feeling that not considering everything is a shortcoming. It can act as a discovery tool for planners to see new opportunities that can enhance their success. And inquirers can simply ask for clarification on how an idea plays out, not as a challenge, but simply to help them understand. This helps planners double-check their thinking through explanation rather than as a rebuttal.

We find that the framework is very useful for helping shift conversations from a "but" response to an "and" response as people can focus on where effort can help add value. It also helps planners see when an area of effort really doesn't create any value or serves no purpose other than following what has traditionally been done.

The framework can also be helpful in building bridges between functions and initiatives. When one team is describing what it intends to do, members can use the framework as a way of presenting the team's approach and describing what the inputs and outputs of their efforts are likely to be—and what kind of experience and value this is intended to yield. This can help spread opportunity and allow others to benefit from the effort, and it can also help seed the request for support, because there is room for negotiation before the situation becomes dependent on meeting a unilateral requirement.

One way to approach this is to identify existing and intended initiatives and plot them on the framework. This can be as simple as creating a Gantt-style bar that represents activities and experiences within or across stages, or it can be a more complex graphing of which emotional and pragmatic needs of the customer are being targeted and supported, which touch points are used, and who is managing or delivering the experience. Planners and teams should adopt and adapt these tools in ways that make the most sense for their business and customers; the framework we provide here should be a guide, as we would rather see new ways that work than have them narrow their approach simply because they couldn't use a particular version of a tool.

Storyboards of what should happen across stages illustrate how experience concepts function and interrelate. Service design–level blueprinting that specifies data flows, business rules, and business roles helps planners see which initiatives have interdependencies with others, which ones should actually be more seamless to the customer, and which ones would benefit from being consolidated or integrated.

The purpose is to help think through what the customer is likely to need and how the customer will perceive actions taken by the business to help meet those needs. The goal is to remove gaps and discontinuities of service or quality of experience, with the ideal state being a less fragmented experience for the customer.

One last example for using the customer journey framework (for sharing views and efforts) is the way it can function as a dashboard for what the business is currently doing and where it wants to improve. When it's used for auditing the existing customer experience, which we will explain in the next section, the results can be plotted using simple techniques such as red, orange, and green bars to represent the effectiveness of each part of the experience. The result is a simple graphical representation that can help executives and functional managers understand what's going on and evaluate where effort should be focused.

This can be approached in a number of ways. One would be to do a qualitative assessment, where observation and interviews with employees and customers would inform an analysis of experiences at touch points. Another would be using quantitative methods and actual data of metrics that are considered important to maintain at certain benchmarks. A lot of the determination of which approach to take would be based on how easy it is to conduct the assessment, how important accuracy and granularity are to managing the process, and how much effort will be placed on correcting problems and maintaining levels of service. We believe that at least some base-level assessment on a quarterly or semiannual basis would allow planning to determine whether new initiatives are likely to be successful or if existing issues will be potential risks that need to be addressed in order to gain the maximum benefit.

A real-world example of this came up when a client was considering redesigning the packaging for its products. A key issues was how the package and out-of-box experience (what it's like to unbox and begin using a product) contributed to perceptions of Brand value. One big financial question was whether to include the printed user manual, which added to the cost of goods and shipping expenses, or whether to provide an electronic version on a CD. There were two camps: One thought that the manual was so important that not including a physical copy would reduce the value of the product; the other thought that significant cost reductions could be achieved by using a less expensive approach. By interviewing clients and seeing how they used the product and what they thought of its packaging, it became clear that the issue was not whether or not a physical manual was important. The real issue was that the manual was often incorrect and customers generally used third-party manuals because they were of higher quality and more effectively showed how to use the product to meet their needs.

Auditing Existing Practices

The customer journey framework can be a very useful tool for guiding and presenting the findings and analysis of experience audits. An audit is simply a mapping of what is currently happening. The thoroughness of an audit is tied to what you hope to learn from it, but in general, usefulness and thoroughness are tightly coupled. One challenge for conducting audits is ensuring that people actually look at the right components of the experience. The customer journey framework can serve as the index from which an audit can be conducted. By defining which areas should be considered and what is important in that area, those conducting the audit can be sure to collect information that is appropriately granular or not, thereby ensuring the analysis is of more use.

One approach is to conduct a benchmark analysis where experiences of a business and its competitors are audited and compared to see how they stack up against each other and to determine what is considered a minimum level of quality and value. This can help business and design see where improvements need to be made to achieve parity and where efforts would potentially create a higher level of value or would produce significant differentiation.

Another approach is to look at the experiences provided by market leaders to identify what they are doing and how they are doing it. A business would undertake such an audit not only to identify and help close gaps in its approach but also to understand how there might be an advantage in differentiating and on what basis.

A variation of this can also be useful: A company can audit another business in a different vertical or sector to understand how that company is delivering a successful customer experience. In this situation, the goal is not necessarily to follow or copy the experience exactly, but to learn from it and see how these lessons might apply to the business's approach to its customers, products, and services. Interesting innovations often start out in one industry and then migrate over time to others. The audit approach allows a business to potentially identify emerging practices and breakout practices in other industries before its industry or sector adopts them.

As we mentioned in the previous section, there is also a lot of value in ongoing auditing of the experience that a business provides to its customers. Using the customer journey framework can make this process easier to manage, because it can provide a consistent template for approaching audits over time. It can also provide a universal template that departments can use for auditing across their functions, while allowing for easy integration of findings across departments.

For any kind of audit, the best approach is to show examples of the experience. This can include photos, videos, flowcharts, interview transcripts, and even SWOT (strengths, weaknesses, opportunities, threats) analyses for given touch points, products, services, experiences, and environments—literally any component of the experience.

Developing a large format of a customer journey framework and then putting these examples in place really helps people understand what the experience is like and highlights disparities across the experience (for example, "Yes, it was a wonderful trade show, but the follow-up material was next to useless!"). We have often taken up entire walls of large conference rooms to plot out experiences, but it can also be done in more portable formats. The point is that it is important for people to see how things work over time and understand upstream and downstream interdependencies because this is how the customer actually experiences things.

It's interesting to watch the "aha!" and "wow!" moments that happen when you have a group of department heads together to review the total experience a customer is having across all of their efforts and areas of responsibility. We are always surprised at how fast people decide what changes should be made and how willing they are to take responsibility for changes when they see customer experiences laid out this way.

Generating and Extending Value Concepts

We find that the customer journey framework is an extremely useful and valuable tool for experience design during the product and service definition phase. It reinforces the concepts of using information, looking at different opportunities to differentiate experiences, and helps organize ideas that lead to innovation.

We typically approach this in one of two ways. One way is using the framework for teasing out new ideas and concepts; the second is for extending existing ideas and concepts.

In the first approach, we find that using an associative or lateral thinking exercise is a good starting point. There is a range of techniques for this kind of brainstorming or idea development; any of them can be a good place to start, depending on the nature of the ideas you are looking to generate, the team size, and the skill sets and level of experience represented. We suggest using customer research or market/trend analysis reports; when combined with tools such as the needs and value proposition framework or the trend and implication framework from Chapter 6, they provide a good starting point.

We find that once initial ideas start flowing, it's easy to generate quantity—it can be more difficult to find quality. Often, it helps to have some kind of springboard or filter that focuses ideas that may initially be inspired by a more open-field ideation technique.

The three that we often use are:

> Brand concept/Brand value pillars: Look for ideas that naturally align to categories of value that are extensions of the Brand concept. You can also refine ideas or recast them against a value category.

> Existing pain points in the customer journey: Knowing where you should be focusing efforts can also help filter ideas effectively and help people who have a strong commitment to an idea recast it to meet an existing need.

> Business goals: Obviously, revenue generation and growth are important, and sometimes these require shifts in approaches or new strategic objectives. These can be effective for helping prioritize ideas or revise an existing idea in such a way that a revenue model can be identified.

Once an idea or concept has been identified, vetted, and in some cases, refined, we place it on the framework based on where it seems to have the most application (that is, where it's likely to be most relevant in terms of creating value in an experience for a customer). The value proposition and use context tool can help identify where in the journey a particular idea or concept would be most effective for existing customers. It can also be used to define where and how a given idea is likely to provide value to a prospective customer.

The process involves extending, refining, connecting, consolidating, and refining again. We find that quick rounds of iterations using tools such as storyboards and scenarios, all at a sketch level, allow multiple stakeholders to understand what is being done and provide additional input in the form of information, insight, or direction for specific revisions. We often treat these storyboards and scenarios as possible "scenes" that can easily be rearranged, edited, and inserted into other scenarios to support a need. The process can be analogous to editing a film, but the difference is that you don't need to go out and reshoot if you don't like a take; you simply revise that section of the storyboard.

A last step before presenting to broader groups and stakeholders is to prioritize the ideas. Final ideas can then be evaluated against a range of criteria. These should be tied to some basic categories, such as how well an idea helps support a strategic business objective, how much value it creates for the customer, how well it strengthens the Brand, and how difficult (in terms of time, skill, and money) it will be to implement. We also suggest developing a road map that illustrates the intended order of design, development, and deployment based on needs, risk management, logical interdependencies, level of effort, and expected benefit.

As we described earlier, the framework itself can also be used as a graphic tool to communicate how these ideas work and why they are of value, which is key to gaining internal approval and support and ensuring that the ideas integrate with other efforts.

The entire concept of this kind of journey framework can be used at different levels of granularity, and of course, this extends all the way down to task flows for product and service features. This is a common practice of many user-centered design processes. What we think is unique about experience design is taking the process back out to the macro-level view and thinking about the larger stages that a product or service sits within, as this is often not done or is difficult for teams to do when focused on tactical definitions and design. But it's this back and forth of perspective shifting that can bring new insights to the tactical decisions that can make a significant difference in the value a customer perceives and how it is differentiated. We believe that this is where business and design can truly make changes that matter.

165

8

Putting It Together

We hope that by this point that there are lights coming on in many readers' heads about how they should change the way that they look at their business and their customers. We hope that there is some recognition of how experience design presents different ways in which business and design can begin collaborating.

Of course, it is easy for us, as evangelists of this approach, to be deeply familiar with all the nuances and ways of connecting different parts of the frameworks and tool kits. We have seen the need for this way of thinking for some time and have been trying to move our teams, our clients, and our business to be better positioned to put this into action. But before we close the door on this section it's probably useful to spend a little time trying to wrap the thinking together to help clarify any questions.

In Chapter 4 we introduced a model for thinking about Brand as arising from a business's strategy, expression of intent, value put into the market, and the engagement people have with the business. We would like to revisit that construct briefly to illustrate how the frameworks and tools we have just shown in the three preceding chapters can be used to integrate Brand, experience, and value.

Figure 8.1 is the diagram that we used to illustrate how the actual experiences people have over time with any business (the circle) is a reflection of all the activities and efforts across the corners of the Brand diamond.

—

Figure 8.1
Brand as Arising from All of a Business's Activities

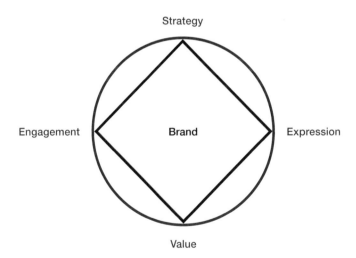

Figure 8.2 shows how the different aspects of the frameworks and tools that we have introduced in this section are integrated through an experience design approach.

Experience design is predicated on the idea that a Brand has to be connected to value as perceived by the customer to have any real meaning and true benefit to the business. Brand concept and Brand value pillars are used to convert the basic essence of the Brand from an abstraction into actionable areas that inform what kind of value can be created for customers. This activates the Brand and makes it available to everyone in the business to use as a guide and a tool. It also helps create a stronger meaning in the minds of customers, as now they may have an explicit understanding of what the Brand concept means in their everyday lives.

Experience design is also based on an approach to Brand experience that believes that Brands cannot be only skin-deep. For a Brand to really exist, it must be brought to life in each experience that the customer has with the business behind the Brand. This needs to be more significant than a consistent use of a logo or a particular messaging vocabulary or attitude. Brand attributes transform the Brand from a shallow, static identity system that is largely used for consistent recognition, into the DNA that can be used to guide the development of artifacts, behaviors, and qualities of experience that apply to every aspect of the customer experience. In this way Brand attributes can now enable a level of coherency that helps deliver true differentiation, while being flexible enough to influence the qualities of the experiences customers have anywhere in their journey of engagement with the business.

Experience design provides the frameworks and tools through which products and services can be evaluated based on the true requirements that are most likely to affect how customers perceive value. The experience design approach acknowledges the role of standard human-factors concerns supported by user-centric design approaches and the importance of desirability and emotional drivers that are identified by design thinking methodologies. Experience design frameworks and tools expand the consideration of value beyond the expected steps of usability and desirability in order to address situations that are more complex. For instance, many parts of an experience may not be directly within control of the business, or market pressures may make it impossible for a company to wait until every feature has been developed before launching its product or service. Finally, the product and service frameworks and tools also help explore the areas in which needs will be emerging and help guide how existing relationships or changes in the broader business context give rise to new needs that may be the best way to evolve a business and Brand.

We believe that one of the most important aspects of experience design is the ability to help business and design think from a customer perspective. Experience design reminds us that products and services are not experienced and evaluated in a vacuum. They are part of a continuous set of activities and are always in a context that is influenced and affected by upstream and downstream experiences a customer has with a business. Experience design helps business and design avoid the mistake of not realizing this until it has a detrimental effect on the customer experience. The customer journey framework is a tool that supports this thinking and propels the thinking beyond the strengths (and limitations) of design methodologies. It can break down functional silos within the business and provide a broad context in which to discuss the relationship between strategy and tactics. We believe that this is a crucial part of an approach to growing business through engaging customers, which is highly flexible and allows for lower risk.

—

Figure 8.2
An Integrated Framework of Experience Design

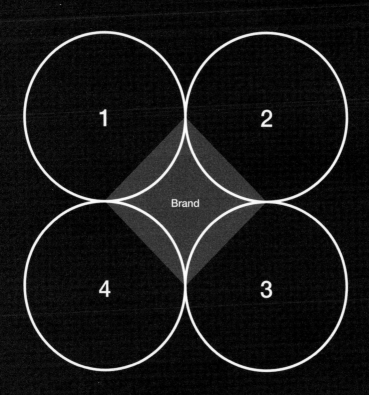

1	2	3	4
Brand Concept and Value Pillars	**Brand Attributes**	**Products and Services**	**Customer Journey**
A translation of the Concept into categories that define true value for customers	A way to bring the qualities of the Brand to life through artifacts and behaviors that differentiate, and are part of real value for customers	How the company meets the needs of customers in ways that provide real value	The stages of engagement and qualities of experience that customers have while trying to engage with a business in order to receive value and satisfy needs

One of the underlying aspects of experience design that differentiates it from other approaches that attempt to be holistic in addressing engagement between customer and business is how time plays such a crucial role. This begins at the atomic level in how products or services need to be thought of over time. People's needs and perceptions of value change over time. Defining and designing the steps involved in using a product feature is not the same as thinking about how the user's frame of mind will change over time as he or she uses a product or service in real everyday life.

At a broader level, a consistent application of Brand and messaging across touch points from marketing through point-of-sale through out-of-the-box experience is not the same as understanding how the rational and emotional mind-set of a customer shifts as the individual goes through this experience. Business and design need to anticipate how and where gaps and problems can crop up that will undermine a customer's confidence in his or her decisions and erode that person's perceptions of value in the purchases being made. Social media strategies, call centers, and customer relationship management programs do not guarantee that you are truly engaging customers in ways that add value and are likely to keep them interested and actively engaged with your business. All of these are useful channels, but simply operating them is not a guarantee that they are providing relevant value to customers and thereby making the Brand the logical first choice for customers when they are seeking out solutions to emerging needs.

At the broadest level, experience design works across all stages of the business life cycle. The basic principles, as well as the frameworks and tools, can help start-up businesses focus on aligning efforts when time, money, and resources are all in short supply. It also helps mid-cycle companies improve their performance by identifying where poor customer experiences have developed through ad hoc decisions made as a result of rapid growth, competitive pressures, or product and service proliferation (often the result of mergers or acquisitions). Finally, experience design provides ways for mature companies to explore new areas of value. It can help identify and deliver innovations to customers or extend the Brand into new areas of value that are required because of changing technology or shifts in what customers need and expect.

Section III
Moving Forward

Perfection of means and confusion of ends seems to characterize our age.

–Albert Einstein[1]

We once sat in on a pitch where one of the world's leading brand consultancies was talking with a software company about what should happen with the company's brand. The consultants discussed the importance of making the brand part of the overall culture and not just the domain of marketing and communications. To make the point, the consultant talked about the impression he had while visiting the Nike campus (corporate headquarters). From the other side of the table, one of the executives from the software company cut in and said, "I was a creative director at Nike. Wieden+Kennedy owns the Nike brand." No engagement came out of the pitch. Another larger software company bought the first software company a few years later, and the latter's brand was fully digested within the acquirer.

We have always liked this story. We aren't saying it's true that Nike's brand is owned by an agency, but we believe that as an example, it's illustrative of the kind of relationships that exist between a business, its brand, and how it approaches working with design. We think business will always benefit from a relationship with design. The question is: What underpins this relationship, and how does it help create more value from the collaboration, rather than a potential asymmetrical relationship where either business constrains what design can really do to help create value or where business is no longer in control of how its value is positioned to the market? The problem with the former situation is that the customer experience can degrade and suffer without anyone necessarily being in a position to see or change this. The problem with the latter is that the ability to see where and why to change what value the customer wants or needs, especially as the larger environment shifts, may be obscured.

We propose that by adopting an experience design–centric view of the world, businesses may be in a better position to understand what areas of value are most connected to their brands and be able to effectively use design to understand why something can be of more value and how it can be delivered in ways that engage the customer.

It's easy enough to take an objective stance and criticize a process or point out problems in the way something is being approached. It's a whole different thing to actually try to maintain that objective perspective when in the midst of the challenges of running a successful business. So much of what we do as humans is influenced by what we have done in the past, what we believe is expected and most efficient, and what we believe will be most successful—but not necessarily with a fresh analysis. It can often be very difficult to understand if what we're doing is wrong or if the way we're going about accomplishing it is wrong. As a result, it can be difficult to know when change is needed, especially if we're doing what everyone else is doing and many of them seem to be successful in their endeavors.

In the book *Being Wrong: Adventures in the Margin of Error*, the journalist, author, critic, and TED speaker Kathryn Schulz points out that the problem stems from not knowing when we're wrong—we don't know what it's like to be thinking incorrectly—we only know what it's like to realize that we were wrong[2]. We'd also suggest the opposite way of looking at this: If there are a bunch of really smart people coming up with a solution to a problem, how can they be sure which solution is right? As Samuel Arbesman reminds us, our information has a half-life and is continually decaying, so even if we're sure we are right because our thinking rests on the facts, the facts themselves may change.

One of the biggest challenges that any design process can face is communication. People coming together on a project may have different backgrounds, areas of expertise, and familiarity with and expectations of the design process. If some of

UNIVERSITY OF WINCHESTER
LIBRARY

these people are only involved sporadically or at specific stages, there is no opportunity for a shared lexicon to develop. Rather than feeling like they are part of a successful collaboration, people may wind up frustrated, feeling that they were not able to successfully contribute. Using a common framework that can be applied across projects and continues to be useful overtime can help make communication more effective. We think that if this can be done in a way that ensures more value for the customer as well, all the better.

This final section is intended to help equip businesspeople and designers with ideas for changing the way they approach a collaborative relationship, assuming that experience design has resonated with them in some way. It's not a change management guide, and it's not necessary to adopt everything we are saying here— it's more of a primer for integrating experience design in your day-to-day responsibilities. We would bet that there are already people within every business who would say that they're looking at the world this way. We know that there are design service providers who do.

We hope that this section will help identify how to leverage these thinkers and help transition the processes and the overall understanding and evaluation of how business and design collaborate to create better value for and engagement with customers.

9

Getting Business to Act on Experience Design

We have purposefully taken a broad approach to describing experience design, largely because we want to present it as a mind-set that can inform how problems can be framed and approached. We don't think it should be simply viewed as a specific strategy with a tactical initiatives checklist that a business might choose to implement. Part of this is due to the nature of the problems it is intended to address—these things change over time. Having the right systems, tools, and basic concepts that can be adapted to meet new requirements provides for a higher level of flexibility and, hopefully, a longer life span in providing value to business and design. The other reason for this is our intentions for this book—to start a conversation about the challenges facing business, design, Brand, value, and experience, and to help move people away from what we believe are dated and inefficient approaches to solving these problems. We aren't saying there is only one way to do things.

We do want these ideas to move beyond the confines of this book, because we strongly believe that acting on this thinking will be beneficial to businesses and their customers. So now we will focus a little more narrowly to provide some useful ways for people to begin using what we have presented so far. Because there are probably more people involved in business than in design, much of this chapter will assume that the context in which the reader is considering using experience design is within a business, not a studio.

Initiating a New Way of Thinking

Designing, developing, and managing the entire customer experience is no small task, even for small organizations. At the heart of the problem is the reality that building great experiences is everyone's responsibility and nobody's job. When one considers how businesses are organized and what tends to be most important—the bottom-line financial performance—discussing new ways of thinking about Brand, value, and experience doesn't always have a ready audience, let alone a universal platform for evaluating different schools of thought. But part of our thinking on experience design is that businesses need to realize that it's on their shoulders to initiate a change in perspective, because their future is at stake.

There are two general approaches to creating change: top-down and bottom-up; neither way works perfectly by itself. Generally, targeting somewhere in the middle and working both up and down seems to produce results a bit faster. With either a top-down or a bottom-up approach, at some point the question has to be asked: Is it more efficient to move thinking first in order to influence actions, or the other way around?

If you can see value in change, then change is worth pursuing. Making incremental change that can yield benefits at each stage is probably easier than trying to change everything all at once. The question may be what amount of change makes sense and why. Knowing this will help you determine a course of action.

One approach to take is to shift the way that people think about problems. Moving thinking this way is important, because it can create some momentum that helps broader change begin to come about. The issue with moving thinking, as opposed to action, is that it may take longer, which can result in people getting stuck in navel-gazing or debates. For instance, some people may argue that being first, building quick wins, focusing on maximizing margins, and creating a convincing business story and valuation are more important than spending a lot of time focusing on Brand, perceived value, and customer engagement. We still argue for a role for experience design; having a plan for Brand, value, and engagement isn't going to hurt, and it might even make the overall value of the business stronger.

On the other hand, jumping into action can become a problem for creating a longer-term change. If time is a constraint, it can be difficult to overcome old habits (and inertia) without first providing both the broader context for a new approach and clear tactical steps for a relatively narrow application of the thinking. There can be challenges to the expertise and authority of those suggesting such changes, and some people will simply miss the forest for the trees and fail to understand why short-term change is important to meeting a long-term goal. In addition, if implementing an experience design approach fails or is not immediately successful (or at least more successful than previous approaches), its value can easily be discounted and any associated thinking may not be considered again.

The challenge comes in identifying where one might apply effort and expect to get the most movement if one were to start pushing. We are proponents of looking for areas where there is either already similar thinking that can be enhanced through input and support or problems that seem to have lost their way and might benefit from fresh approaches. In both cases the goal should be to help create small successes that can shift thinking.

One of the reasons that books such as *The Wide Lens* and *The Price of Fish* strike us as being so significant is that they take a systems view or apply a networked model to things, which we think is the way much of the world should be approached. It also makes sense when introducing experience design into a business. In every business, multiple systems and networks are operating—management and reporting networks, processes and operations networks, go-to-market and market-response networks, strategic level and tactics-level networks, and formal and informal networks.

A good starting point for planning how to introduce experience design is to think about these systems and networks:

- Which systems adapt to changes faster, and which ones are more entrenched in convention?

- Within any system, who would provide the most impetus to change, and what would be that person's or group's incentive?

- What are the risks and impediments to that person or group acting?

- Has the person or group bought in to the basic principles experience design already? If so, to what degree?

- What other systems are likely to be affected?

- Within these affected systems, who has to adopt and implement the change?

- How do these people benefit? What are the risks and impediments to their acting?

- What are the real power networks that determine what information is considered and influence decision making?

- Which informal communications networks tend to have the biggest impact on what happens in the formal communication networks?

Regardless of how or where you want to start looking in order to develop an experience design mind-set within a business, be prepared for an ongoing process. It's not a one-time switch but more of a shift in what should be included under the general art and science of business. It will take time for businesses to internalize and intuitively act on the understanding of how design can play an instrumental part in creating value for customers. It is still too easy to leave design as the last step.

In general, the broader the point of view, the longer it takes to fully understand, internalize, and begin to use it in day-to-day thinking. But our theory is that people are curious and want to be successful with less effort. Showing and sharing success will benefit work more than mandating new processes.

Starting the Conversation about Experience Design

Building a groundswell of advocacy may be the best way to introduce experience design within an organization. People need exposure to any new idea or perspective before they can begin to consider how it might change their way of seeing the world. Balancing efforts to educate with efforts to find those who already understand and practice this approach can create the most leverage and efficiency.

Even if most principles, arguments for, and tools of experience design resonate with people, there's still a barrier to overcome. Does it make sense in the case of a specific individual to put the ideas behind experience design into action given that person's sense of the cost versus benefit of doing so? We suggest that instead of trying to convince people that they need to start thinking differently and help the business adopt an experience design mind-set, it is often easier to look at the problems or opportunities facing the business. These often provide a better context for introducing the thinking, frameworks, and tools of experience design in ways that help solve the problems and issues the staff see. It's always easier to adopt something that you have used and found value in than to simply take it on faith.

We have developed a list of primary questions that pertain to different business contexts that have proved to be good starting points for talking about an experience design approach. Each primary question is followed by a brief description of the problem that may have given rise to the question. This is followed by a list of more detailed questions that might help fully answer the primary question.

How can we convince our customers that the product or service we're developing is valuable?

Business cases can be made based on fairly high-level descriptions of needs and value propositions. It is during the definition, design, and development stages that a finer level of detail becomes crucial; otherwise, decisions that support the high-level business case but not the customer may be made. The problem here is that if the customer chooses not to buy, the business case doesn't pan out.

The kind of detailed questions that should be answered include:

- Do we really know what the customer's needs are?

- Are we assuming that we think the same way the customer does?

- Who are the most important customers, and how much variation is there in needs across customers for this product or service?

- Do we understand which needs are likely to drive the customer to buy our product over another?

- Do we think that these are long-term needs, or are there other needs that become more important to fulfill to keep the customer satisfied?

- How is the work being done to ensure that value for the customer exists in the product or service being informed by or influencing other things we are doing (such as marketing, sales, support)?

- How do we know if a customer is satisfied?

- How are we defining and designing the product or service in a way that is truly a reflection of our Brand and is different from what another business would decide to do?

- What are we using as a model for usable life span of the product or service, and how do we keep a customer engaged throughout?

- How do we make and evaluate decisions if we lack information or are uncertain about what will be important in the future?

Our primary source of revenue is service-based. What is our customer experience strategy?

When service is a big component of the business model, it's important to always remember that customers' perception of value is tightly coupled with their satisfaction and willingness to continue using a service. The kind of detailed questions that should be answered include:

- Do we know what our customers consider the most valuable part of our service?

- What are we doing to grow value in these areas?

- Do we have a competitive advantage in these areas, and is it sustainable?

- How quickly would our business erode if we lost that advantage?

- What's the first sign that we will see when we no longer have an advantage?

- How will we react to this situation?

- What other areas of value can we introduce and focus on?

Our main source of revenue is monetizing an audience. What are our strategies for customer engagement and retention?

Many services and sources of value are "free" to customers because providers make money by selling the data, attention, or access to the people who use the service. But if there is value for users of the service, they may not be taking the rational position of managing their expectations against what they have paid. If a competitor can offer the same value for free, then it makes no real difference that the customer is not paying. The kind of detailed questions that should be answered include:

- What keeps people coming to our service?

- How can we help them discover more value?

- How can we provide more value for them?

- What are the ways that helping discover more value and providing more value can also drive our revenue model beyond raw numbers of audience size or growth?

How broad and varied are our customers, and what does this suggest about our products and services and the future of our business?

When customer needs are fairly homogenous, it can be easier to keep everyone satisfied than when the needs and expectations are more varied. When faced with varying needs and expectations, it is key to know which variables are the most important. It's also important to think beyond just the end user and understand all the roles that may go into a decision to buy. There may be customers who are rarely "seen" but who have the most clout. The kind of detailed questions that should be answered include:

- How do we get a better understanding of our customer?

- Who are our most valuable customers and why?

- How do we make a customer more valuable?

- What do we need to do to prevent valuable customers from decreasing in value?

- What are differences in the customer journeys for the different kinds of customers that are important to the business?

- How does technology affect the channels and touch points used for supporting the customer journeys?

- Are channels integrated across customer journeys?

- How much visibility do we have across channels, and how is this being used to create more value and drive deeper engagement?

- What opportunities might exist to create new revenue streams based on customers' preferred use of channels?

How much direct competition do we face, and how does it affect our business strategy?

In highly competitive markets, differentiation can be extremely important, yet real differentiation is hard to do well. Youngme Moon cites examples of businesses that have taken differentiation strategies very seriously and discussed how it has an effect on everything the company does, including what it decides not to do.[1] Hoping to differentiate at the customer experience level alone is challenging to pull off, but differentiating across the board needs to be exceptionally well coordinated to effectively engage customers. Another way of saying this is: Doing the same thing in a slightly different way may not make a difference. Making a truly different offering still requires meeting the threshold of perceived value and engagement. The kind of detailed questions that should be answered include:

- What is our differentiation strategy?

- How do we know that it is working, and what metrics are the best to use?

- How do we use it to define, design, and deliver products, services, and experiences?

- How is this tied to our Brand concept?

- Do we have customers who are advocates and evangelists?

- How do we benefit from them and acknowledge their support?

- How do we help people become advocates and evangelists?

What is the likelihood that customers will lose interest in our products or services?

Many products and services have successful early adoption because of the novelty and the momentum that early adoption can bring, but this doesn't necessarily translate to long-term customer use. In some cases the true value is tied to a network effect, so continuing to grow, especially across relevant connections for customers, is crucial. In other cases, it may be that the value of a product or service goes only so far, and there needs to be subsequent or adjacent value for engagement to continue. The kind of detailed questions that should be answered include:

- Do we have a customer journey model?

- When do customers usually stop buying and why?

- What do we usually do when this happens?

- How effective is this kind of response?

- What could make it more effective?

What risk do disruptive technologies pose to our business?

The promise of technology is often accompanied by the real risk of permanent erosion of a business model. Sometimes this is readily apparent at the outset; other times it is slower to appear. The kind of detailed questions that should be answered include:

- What technologies help us reduce costs, and how can these also help us provide more value for customers?

- What technologies are important to our customers but have not been adopted yet?

- How can we use these technologies to our benefit?

- How are the benefits organized in terms of customer engagement, retention, and revenue?

- Are revenues incremental additions to existing revenues or replacing existing revenues?

- How does the scale of adoption of benefits affect revenue growth?

- Are there new business models that arise from providing benefits from new technologies to existing customers?

- What is the value chain, and who are the true customers for these new business models?

- How should introduction of new technologies and transition of business models be handled?

How much Brand awareness and relevance do we have with the new customer segments that are important to our future?

As businesses grow, new markets can become attractive. In other cases existing markets may simply be decreasing, making viability dependent on attracting new customers. In either case the awareness and equity of a Brand may not be as fungible as the business might like it to be, necessitating the bridging of Brand meaning and value that allows access to new markets without alienating existing markets. The kind of detailed questions that should be answered include:

- What does the Brand (concept) mean?

- How is the Brand being brought to life?

- Do the products and services really deliver value that reinforces the meaning of the Brand?

- What kinds of things (values and beliefs) are important to customers in new markets and new market segments?

- How can this knowledge be used to understand needs and create value that leverages our Brand meaning?

How much do we rely on products or services from other businesses to make our value proposition real for customers?

More and more products and services function as components of a solution. Sometimes this is the intent of the provider(s), and sometimes customers simply have created their own solutions to their needs through the use of a variety of products and services. These can be both opportunities for business and areas of risk. The opportunity is that you may be able to provide value to a customer by enhancing a solution that the customer has begun to use. The risk is that your solution, or your role in a solution, may be contingent on the products and services of others. The kind of detailed questions that should be answered include:

- Which products or services are our customers most likely to use in conjunction with ours?

- What is the relationship and value hierarchy between our products and services and these others?

- What are the primary areas of risk or weakness?

- How do we change this to our advantage?

- How does a customer usually get exposed to these, assuming an idealized customer journey?

- How should the customer be exposed to these so that we can provide higher value and get deeper engagement?

- Who does our business rely on to provide value and enhance solutions (for example, third-party developers, partners, other products and services)?

- Who provides support for customers in these situations, and how fragmented is the customer's access to and experience with support?

- Where are the major gaps?

- What incentives do partners have to maintain and grow value and quality of service and experiences?

- What is the potential for a partner to become a competitor?

- What makes it likely that a customer would defect in such a situation?

What is the potential for cross-selling and up-selling products and services to an existing customer?

Many business-to-business (B2B) Brands have multiple products and services, and in many cases these cover different areas of need for the same customer. In some cases these are tied to extending and integrating value propositions for existing needs; in other cases they may be tied to or contingent on helping the customer move into new products and services for their end customers (we call this closing the value gap).

For business-to-consumer (B2C) Brands, technology and channel integration are making it possible to provide new or additional services (such as the cable/phone/ISP triple-play model or the banking account services/brokerage/financial products model) to customers. The kind of detailed questions that should be answered include:

- Do we have a direct relationship with the customer?

- Who owns the relationship with the customer?

- Is the customer aware of this relationship? If so, how does the customer use it?

- What is the nature and quality of this relationship?

- How complex are the purchase decisions for new products and services?

- What are the barriers to buy or adopt?

- Where do these exist in the customer journey, and what's the best way to help our customer get past them?

- What's the likelihood that another business would be acquired in order to provide additional products and services to existing customers?

- How will the customer experience the integration?

- Will the customer's understanding of who is providing value change?

- What is the impact of this on other areas of the customer relationship?

Many of these are based on real situations we have encountered with clients. There are several ways that these questions can be used.

One approach is to ask executives and decision makers all or most of the primary questions. This is a way of gauging how important customer value and engagement are to their view of the business. The answers can then be collected and used to build a case for a better foundation on which to move forward into the future. It doesn't necessarily ask them to adopt an experience design perspective, but it does begin to open up a discussion of some of the areas that might benefit from such a perspective.

A second approach is to use a specific primary question that relates to a program, product, or area of the business. Ask the secondary questions as a way of beginning to see how equipped managers and teams are for framing the problems they need to address. If people agree that they are important points but can't give strong answers, it's likely that they will benefit from using some of the thinking, frameworks, and tools of experience design.

A last way would be to use the list in conjunction with people who are existing or likely advocates to build a broader sense of where to target change efforts or focus on persuading others to begin to incorporate new ways of looking at existing needs.

Creating Leverage

Over the years, we have met many people who are aligned with much of the thinking we describe within experience design. These are people from other design and strategy studios, people within our clients' organizations, business leaders, journalists, and pundits. It is likely that most companies have many such individuals, and we believe that through conversations and inquiry based on the preceding lists, or even through discussing aspects of this book, you will quickly identify them in your business as well. Identifying, working with, and enabling these people as advocates for experience design—sharing the thinking and the approaches discussed—can help move businesses toward a better internal understanding of experience design and create more efficiency in collaborating with design to create the successes and proof points that can lead to deeper change.

There are several ways that advocates can be enabled and supported.

Internal Experience Design Council

Creating a more formal group with a clear focus and agenda can help bring individual advocates together. Part of the benefit here is letting people know that they are not alone, thereby strengthening relationships by spreading success stories and useful knowledge and allowing for faster access to information and practices across departments and functional roles.

Such a group should decide on its objectives and, based on availability and the overall need of the business, determine how much they intend to do and over what kind of time frame. For example, a first step may be for two like-minded people to try to establish a monthly meeting with the goal of adding one additional recruit per month.

Some of the objectives that might be worth consideration are listed here. We also suggest that these be approached from a level of need/level of effort basis so that efforts don't get stalled because plans are overambitious. These efforts could include the following:

Structured advocacy efforts: The Experience Design Council may decide to enact a formal program of advocacy to create faster change and break down barriers that they believe prevent the business from using an experience design approach to creating value. In addition to generally representing experience design thinking in conversations, discussions, and efforts, this may involve a variety of activities targeted at surfacing and clarifying issues, gaining consensus on the severity of problems, and enlisting and/or brokering support or buy-in from individuals and groups.

Planning: The Experience Design Council may take it on themselves to identify an overall approach to issues and problems that they see as risks to business success. This could be a formal plan that would tie in to advocacy efforts with the goal of being adopted company-wide. Or it might also be more informal and reflect the evolution of the business toward being more experience design–minded.

The council may also play a role in the planning processes of others, helping to add a level of experience design thinking to existing programs and projects or helping program and project managers account for experience design in the plans that they need to develop to meet their objectives.

Resource: The Experience Design Council can be a valuable resource of individual experience and expertise that is available for departments and teams. Council members may function as experience design ambassadors and be available to speak to teams and departments and represent experience design thinking in other governing bodies within the business either on an ad hoc or more permanent basis. They can also be tapped to work on specific programs or projects to educate people on the use of frameworks and tools, help provide specific input on problem framing and solving, or observe and evaluate outcomes.

Communication: An Experience Design Council may take on the task of creating and maintaining centralized information systems that help to spread the basic thinking, frameworks, tools, case studies, best practices, and so on. It may decide to start with less systemic approaches and simply provide periodic newsletters, updates, or reports. It can also be a clearinghouse and connection point for information from different parts of the business.

Centralizing Information

As conversations around experience design build momentum and the outcomes of the efforts it influences become more visible, the value of being able to quickly share and distribute information and communicate thinking and progress increases.

If there is a preexisting intranet in the organization, this can be used to centralize information (if one doesn't exist, there are many off-the-shelf and SaaS options worth exploration and implementation). The information can be organized in ways that are most useful to how teams would normally reference this kind of content, but it can also be organized so as to help shift the way a business approaches experience design. Below are a number of options that could be considered.

Brand tools: Having initial thinking about how the Brand concept can be translated into Brand value pillars and how design attributes get used as experience criteria is a useful way to begin to turn the experience design approach into an actionable tool. This may begin as a wiki and then evolve to include actual frameworks and examples of how programs and projects have literally converted the experience design into experience, along with supporting work artifacts.

Advocate network: A social network, or directory of people who have skills and experience working with the concept of experience design, allows people and teams to tap into their perspective and begin conversations that might not have occurred in normal communication systems.

Frameworks and tools: Building repositories of frameworks and tools, including instructions on how to use them, previous examples, and current projects, can also help build peoples' confidence as they adopt these tools. It also helps catalog successes and issues, which can make it easier to pinpoint problems and incorrect usage. This can evolve the effectiveness of tools as they are adapted with a specific business.

Customer journey analyses/dashboards: The customer journey framework can be used to present current information, problems, efforts, and even dynamic metrics. Having such a representation can help spread the thinking even to people who will not have day-to-day needs for the tools and frameworks.

It can also be used within departments to communicate information that may be passing through informal channels but that has no place to be centrally aggregated and evaluated. This could include things such as:

- Where are your customers experiencing the most pain points?

- Where do you and your team plug in?

- What other efforts by the business are you most related to?

- How are you helping them?

- How are they helping you?

Concept/issue maps: It's rare that problems within a business are completely specific to a single group or project. But often these interconnections are not formally mapped—it's all anecdotal information that lives in people's heads. The problems that can occur include:

- People leave the business and no one knows that the knowledge has gone as well.

- People are not sure whom to go to for information or issue resolution.

- Issues grow because of lack of ownership.

- Issues grow because of lack of understanding regarding the volume of problems associated with them.

- Projects and programs stall or fail because issue interdependencies weren't acknowledged or acted upon.

- Assumptions are made that an issue has one implication or meaning when it actually has another.

Concept/issue mapping is similar to mind mapping or semantic mapping. We generally suggest that the relationships be based on causal influence and information interdependence and organized along axes that correspond to timing of efforts and proximity to the customer. One way to think about this is to imagine such a map running up and intersecting with the customer journey framework. All the concepts or issues that need to be identified, developed, and resolved and that affect the customer can be mapped, in order of priority, and all the relationships across the customer journey can be noted. New relationships and issues can be added. We often use three stages of visual alert for concepts and issues:

Red: Serious problems, lack of information, lack of action

Orange: Presence of critical interdependencies

Green: Issue has been resolved and resolution is now available for others to see

Concepts and issues can be defined by elements of programs and initiatives, they can be milestones, they can be assets and documents—essentially they can be any information that is critical for others to be aware of and that may change over time. A variety of people need to know what the information, status, or decisions are around the concept or issue.

A concept or issue can have a variety of levels, but in general we suggest these basics:

General description: What is important and why

Inputs and outputs: What it is affected by and what it affects

Owner: Person or group who is responsible, including stakeholder hierarchies and decision-making process

Timeline: Current schedule of change activities

General information: Documents (such as background reports, research, analysis, requirements), examples (sketches, prototypes or proof-of-concepts), and guidelines (design specifications, data models, information architectures), anything that a downstream concept is dependent on and that an adjacent concept might want visibility into in order to understand the current concept providing the information

Status: Current state of the concept or issue—essentially the reliability of the information it contains and the risks of depending on it, as well as the upstream and downstream problems related to the current status

Idea/innovation networks: Brand value pillars can be used as organizational structures for collecting and providing access to information (for example, news and observations about trends in the business, market, customer needs, technology, etc.), ideas for new products or services, and innovation efforts. This can help to broaden innovation inputs beyond research and development groups and help people understand how design value pillars work to translate the design concept into tangible value for customers.

Enlisting Soft Skills

Whether your advocacy efforts are grass roots, project based, or more formal and hierarchical, it is important to think about some of the skills that might be involved in shifting thinking and helping people understand how to integrate experience design into their everyday mind-set and tool set.

In businesses, people are often measured by specific skills—level of domain expertise, communication skills, general intelligence, ability to manage, all things that are useful for understanding where someone is likely to provide value and excel in a business. But with regard to building advocacy and driving deeper adoption of (and adaptation to) experience design, it's worth looking for other kinds of humanistic skills that make working with complex information and dynamic contexts more fruitful and keep people more engaged.

It's rare to find individuals who exhibit more than a few of these skills (we call those who do "unicorns"). It's not necessary to have each of these skills represented all the time, but it is good to understand how the role they play can aid conversations and identify people who have these skills so that they can be tapped when appropriate. These include:

Catalyzers: These are natural-born hosts and facilitators. Catalyzers possess a high level of empathy and understand interpersonal dynamics, helping them to quickly resolve differences. They thrive on collaboration and like to see teams come together, function efficiently, and be successful.

Contextualizers: Seeing the big picture, these people are constantly zooming from 10 feet to 10,000 feet to see how things are really connected and, from a business point of view, what is interdependent on what. They have access to lots of other people and information. They are good with data and understand the pitfalls of misinterpretations, false-positive results, and misidentification of correlations as causality. They are also uncomfortable with uncertainty when they are certain that the information exists, and they will eventually find it if it does.

Synthesizers: Teasing insights from information and bridging strategy with tactics is the strength of synthesizers. They help go from implication to action and make sure that there is a path that connects value to needs, providing the logical steps of what needs to happen. Synthesizers are strong inductive thinkers and can help make sure that a decent level of specificity can be reached.

Ideaphors: Appropriately fearless, ideaphors are both inspired and inspiring. Naturally creative, they are always able to come up with some thought or reaction that is tied to a piece of information or an area of inquiry. They often ask the most insightful and difficult questions, because they are not necessarily content with the obvious. They help prevent groupthink and tautological solutions.

Storytellers: These are the great communicators who can distill complex and disparate thinking into clear and compelling stories. They are empathetic and ambassadorial, and know how to present the right story for the right audience, while making sure that all the right objectives are equally served. They help make sure that thinking lives on by keeping it accessible and useful through narrative formats that are understandable to a wide audience and are easy to remember and share.

Designophiles: These are people who love good design, know what the trends are, stay up to speed on the latest and greatest design standards, and can represent the broader market context. Ideally, they are also informed enough about design to be able to talk the talk, converse comfortably with real designers, and point out the good and bad of design from a functional and executional perspective, not just personal tastes.

Sequencers: These are the procedural savants, often coming from engineering or technical backgrounds. They excel at seeing problems with logic flows and key interdependencies and are essential to keeping the thinking based on viable and feasible realities.

Visualizers: These are the people who are adept at thinking visually and love to sketch. They can quickly represent any idea in pictures that anyone could easily comprehend with minimal coaching. Ideally, they are familiar with design processes and can be quick stand-ins for tactical designers when it's necessary to do a quick proof of concept for a product or service.

Change and Context Sensitivity

We are not change management experts. None of the ideas we've presented here can remake an organization. But we suspect that when businesses start to think from an experience design perspective, positive change of some kind is inevitable.

We do believe that it is important for businesses to understand that what we are proposing as a way of collaborating with design is not a new form of design process or a different kind of design skill. What we are suggesting is that many of the inefficiencies arise from the ways business frames problems and how and when they engage design to help solve them. From that perspective, it's important for businesses to decide how much change they can and should make. We also suggest that the shift in context of customer, business, and design that we are trying to point out is likely to continue. Businesses that take a different approach to how they use design to help integrate experience design, value, and experience will have a significant advantage in terms of increased ability to react quickly; reduction of risk in defining, designing, and developing products and services; and the ability to more strongly engage with customers.

W connect Aspects
e ES model
ly to oser
fits?

What does energy optimiz-ation bring to your life?

People D
underst
benefi

Benefit
don't fee
tangible
enough

Supporting multiple · users
→ supporting the non · tech person

Y
ization
)

Getting a sense of energy, more than just about

se
Auto-

ited
T

10

Working with Vendors

We would bet that in a random sampling of people around the world, there would be more people who consider themselves nondesigners than people who consider themselves designers. And of those who profess to be designers, only a portion will have the training, skills, and level of experience to be able to make money designing for others. This makes it very probable that most businesses will have some need to collaborate with external designers to address all of their design needs. This is also true for other skills and areas of expertise that businesses need, but because we are primarily concerned with helping business and design collaborate more efficiently through experience design, thinking about how design vendors are engaged is important.

Even if all the people within a business believe in using experience design as a way of creating value for customers, they may still compromise their efforts if they engage with design partners in inefficient ways. And for companies that are unsure of how to approach experience design, changing the way they engage with design partners can make it a lot easier for design to guide them as they put experience design thinking into action.

Much of this comes down to the basics of engagement. There could be an entire volume written about how to plan, look for, hire, work with, and benefit from design partners (and probably one for most other services that a business might outsource). We don't want to redesign the procurement process or dissect every stage of collaboration, but we do want to highlight some areas that we believe will help business and design collaborate more effectively using the approach to experience design that we have introduced.

The points we want to cover apply to three areas: framing of the problem and the "ask" of design, choice of whom to work with and why, and how the financial structuring of the engagement can affect the outcomes.

Avoiding the Basic Problems

Design encounters several issues when collaborating with business on programs and projects, but many of them are directly tied to how the problem is framed and what the expected outcome will be. One of the most common issues is lack of clarity in the actual project objectives. Sometimes this is apparent at the outset, but other times this becomes apparent only as work is progressing when it becomes clear that decisions aren't being made, requirements are changing, or previously established evaluation criteria are being disregarded.

This kind of situation brings up two dynamics, which can become mutually reinforcing and which compromise the overall effectiveness of the outcome. The first of these is what is referred to in economics as the principal-agent problem. The principal hires an agent to act on his or her behalf, but at some point the agent begins to take actions that protect or ensure his or her personal interests rather than those of the principal. If a business makes requests that are unreasonable, within the agreed-upon scope of the engagement, design has a disincentive to fulfill them because they cost the designer and affect profitability. This can be true even if the requests are in the interest of the best solution to the original problem.

The second dynamic that can arise is what might be called the Illusive Design syndrome, in which what is needed can't be adequately defined or described and can be identified only when it is seen.

Most people who are involved in hiring design services would probably feel confident that they would be able to avoid either of these and would definitely be able to prevent them from feeding off each other if they did begin to happen, but these are some of the most basic and prevalent problems that arise when business and design collaborate.

The Brief: Measure Twice, Cut Once

We believe that using a program or project brief is the best first defense against the issues just described. The benefits of a brief are:

- It can be circulated for internal review before it is shared with potential partners.

- It can be updated if the potential partners have questions or ask for a more detailed response.

- It can be used to assess responses in terms of how well they match the brief and what else is recommended or included in the scope of work proposed.

- It can be a point of reference to help manage scope once a program or project has gotten under way.

And, of course, a brief should either implicitly or explicitly provide what success means and how it would be measured.

A brief can also evolve with the project as new information is uncovered, decisions are made, or requirements or product/service definitions are updated. Without this kind of centralized tool, it's easy for the process to get sidetracked, for priorities to inadvertently shift, or even for the entire purpose of the project to fall into question. In the previous chapter, we presented a centralized information tool called the concept/issue map and suggested that this could help in the development of briefs. It can also be useful in providing access across the business to briefs that are being refined and may be important for other efforts to be aware of or able to refer to.

A brief can have many variations, but we believe that from an experience design perspective, there are some basics that will help business and design work more effectively. The beginning point is to frame the problem or objective: What is the collaboration intended to accomplish and why? What is useful here is setting a context that helps establish focus and set expectations regarding the nature of the problem and what might be involved.

A brief should provide the basic backbone of the problem context and demonstrate that there is an understanding of what needs to be addressed. In Chapter 4 we identified three important considerations for an experience design–centric approach:

Consideration 1: Why is this being done, and why is it going to help the business by providing value to customers?

Consideration 2: How is the Brand going to be strengthened by this, and how will the Brand inform the qualities of the value and experience?

Consideration 3: What are the key interdependencies and opportunities?

Figure 10.1
Relationship of Universal Inputs and Project-Specific Inputs
under an Experience Design Approach

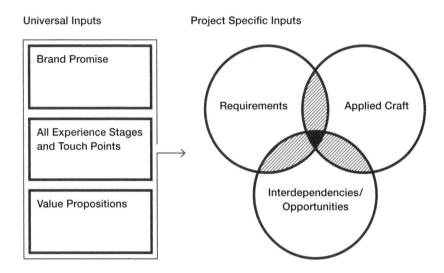

Figure 10.1 repeats a figure from Chapter 4 that is useful in this context. What we suggest is that in framing the problem, business should also specify what design is expected to accomplish and what the relative priority of the different kinds of design outcomes is from the business's perspective. Design's input regarding how to reach the desired project-specific outcomes will be:

- Meeting the general requirements for a solution to the problem

- Enhancing a solution through the application of craft skills

- Supporting known interdependencies or identifying future opportunities

If the expectation from business is that one of these areas is more important than the others and, in fact, the main reason a design partner is being considered, then any efforts that need to be expended by design in service of the other areas are going to create some problems. The misalignment in expectations may lead to scope creep, which can cause a principal-agent problem, or it may have arisen from a lack of adequate information, which can lead to the Elusive Design syndrome. For instance, let's say that a business assumes that all the requirements for a product or service have been thought through, are well defined, and will meet the customer's needs. What business expects is for the design team to apply their skills to make the experience "really special" for the customer.

Now let's say that the requirements are extremely prescriptive and allow for only a very small amount of interpretation. A stakeholder who may not have been familiar with the brief or who may not have paid a lot of attention to it may think the design isn't compelling enough for customers. The product manager may ask design to take another try but keep the requirements as is, preventing design from exploring other avenues. The stakeholder may continue to send the design back. Because the requirements constrain what design can do but the stakeholder is not evaluating against these constraints, the team is stuck in an endless cycle of trying to create something that will be more appealing—an impossible task, unless the requirements change.

A variation of this example is when the business assumes that all the requirements have been thought through and asks design to deliver a compelling solution within a very tight time frame and budget. Then, as the project proceeds, it becomes evident that many requirements are at odds with each other, there is disagreement within the business regarding how to prioritize them, and the design process is ultimately used to explore, clarify, and prioritize the requirements. The time and budget can be spent by the time the requirements are set, yet the business may still expect design to complete the exercise of exploring options and finalizing a chosen direction for the product or service.

In other cases it may simply be that the expectations for the outcome were not adequately clarified. This can happen when a business is looking for a forward-thinking concept or wants to get an external perspective that can be used to inspire internal teams but simply presents the requirements without sharing the big-picture goal. The design team may feel compelled to deliver a solution that interprets the requirements as prescriptive constraints. The business may be disappointed yet unable to specify why, and design may make only minor revisions, afraid to depart from what is thought to be a workable solution.

Another main component of the brief is the identification of what information is available or has been collected and can be used in the process. As we pointed out in Section II, information is a key aspect of good experience design. One of the crucial types of information that is needed for experience design is related to the Brand. Although the brief cannot define the Brand, if information on the Brand does exist, the brief should refer to it to ensure that such information is considered.

Perhaps the one area of a brief that can be most helpful to bringing an experience design thought process into the mix is establishing the role of time (beyond intended project duration). As we explained in laying out the basic principles of experience design, time plays a key role and should be used to think through issues that can help make the brief a better foundation for the collaboration between business and design:

- What potential situations will customers be in, and what would be of most value to them while still aligning with the business goals?

- What most likely preceded the current customer situation, and what are the next steps, driven by customer need, to help further engagement between the customer and the business?

- What other parallel processes or touch points are relevant to consider (including other businesses, products, services, and solutions)?

- What are areas of change outside of the current focus that might influence perceptions of value in the near future?

Even if these are outside the scope of the program or project objectives, providing some reference or explanation helps ensure that teams are aware of these issues. Knowing relevant time horizons in which the outcome is expected to function is important in thinking through relationships to future versions, frequency of use and change in needs for the customer, and likelihood of broader contextual changes for the business, industry, and customer (on this side, one might consider life-stage events or general buying cycles).

We have seen well-structured programs that were months in duration but influenced business activities for years. We have also seen projects that were planned effectively and served multiple stages of the customer journey with the same overall design output simply because these requirements were defined before work began. In the worst case, we have seen a project that failed to acknowledge existing changes in the broader environment and resulted in a product being made irrelevant by changes in the market, before design was complete (and this was a for a product idea proposed by an innovation consultancy!).

Another key aspect of time is considering where the outcome exists on the customer journey, how much of the journey it affects, and what are parallel, dependent, and influencing efforts that the business assumes on behalf of the customer, the products and services, and the partners.

We don't propose that the brief is a perfect snapshot of the past, present, and future, nor do we think that all these areas need to be fully covered for every type of collaboration between business and design. But thinking through which ones are important and deciding which ones are either uncertain or too small in impact will help the brief provide a much better basis for design to ask questions and confidently propose ways of working. It can also help clarify scope and make it easier to see how budgets are constructed to make meeting the objective possible without being wasteful or creating risk by being insufficient for the task.

The examples we listed in this chapter of projects gone awry are all based on real situations, and in all these cases, the one commonality is they had a brief that was overly vague or open-ended. Often, much of the work of design is in getting to a real understanding of the problem and helping create the best framing that can be used to get to a real solution. The brief can help business understand what may be missing, as well as clarify the expectations of what kind of outputs are needed. The time to discover gaps is when reviewing the brief, not when the project is failing.

Many of the frameworks and tools we introduced in Section II can be useful in helping to organize thinking and prepare a brief. But it should also be pointed out that design is very good in facilitating the use of these kinds of frameworks and tools, and perhaps the process should begin with engaging design to help structure the project brief, as opposed to simply taking it as a fait accompli and assuming that it is adequate for informing the process of actually defining, designing, and developing a compelling product or service.

The Business / Design Customer Journey

Eating a bit of our own dog food is going to be helpful to explain two other areas in which business and design can improve the level of collaboration. There are two areas of the design services buyer customer journey that can have a big effect on outcomes and are therefore important to consider. These are Awareness and Consideration, and Purchase.

Awareness and Consideration

Too often the collaboration process begins incorrectly. Many times a business buyer of design services decides to issue an RFP to a wide variety of firms and then seeks to narrow the field down, based on the responses they receive. The complication that this can introduce is an improper framing of the problem and opportunity. This can lead to responses that may not fully address the actual need. There can be a larger variation in how design partners choose to respond, which can make it difficult for the buyer to make a proper evaluation of skills and appropriate fit of potential design partners.

When RFPs are issued to different kinds of firms, the challenge is to identify and compare the strengths and weaknesses of the firms. The initial evaluation is going to start with the contents and quality of the response, but this may or may not be a good indicator of actual skills and ability. It does not really allow for an evaluation of whether or not the design partner is an appropriate fit. It establishes how interesting a candidate's response is, but what is interesting may not necessarily be what is best or needed. We recommend instead conducting initial meetings and issues requests for information (RFIs) to help establish the basic skills, capabilities, and mind-sets of potential partners. Following this up with a well-structured brief will allow you to see how your initial assumptions match specific responses and can help you discern the real differences between recommended approaches.

Often, the RFP process, or just the discussions in general, may be undertaken with multiple motivations on the business side. One of these can be to get some free consulting and a quick survey of thinking to perhaps validate assumptions or make decisions about whether or not an approach makes sense. When a service provider is being asked for an opinion, one of the first things that may enter the provider's head is: What do I stand to gain financially, and what do I need to say to increase my odds? Even if the provider is not conscious of it, someone who is in the seller's seat is more likely to say the things a buyer is going to want to hear, which may not always be the best or correct information. There are few firms that will tell a prospective client that what they are thinking of doing is wrong and will not work, and those that do often simply do it because it is a good sales tactic with some clients.

If you are looking for the highest-quality partners, it's worth investing both time and a little money. Having partners conduct work sessions or execute quick ideation exercises can provide insights into how they think as well as shed some light on what information and approaches are going to be most relevant. It may be that a provider is not the right fit, but you may also realize exactly how best to use that provider to save yourself time and generate more effective thinking in future situations.

Many times, there is a desire to find the right long-term partner, so large RFPs that require proposals that may span a year or more are issued. The time it takes to produce these, conduct the interviews, evaluate the responses, and analyze options can be significant. And many of the issues we have just mentioned can still occur. The worst outcome is to place a huge bet and find out that it was wrong. Although it is harder to accurately plan for the future when smaller steps are being taken, using smaller engagements can often limit the risks and help focus future efforts and reduce costs. It is not uncommon for us to work with clients based on a small fixed-fee stage, which is intended to help scope real needs and establish cost for subsequent stages. The benefit is better flexibility and no obligations to continue if for any reason the fit is wrong.

One last problem that arises in this stage of the buyer's journey is the assumption that all design is the same. This generally occurs because of the challenge of semantics. When a design firm says it creates Brands, business buyers may assume that means anything and everything related to a Brand, when, in fact, it may mean that the firm designs identity marks. A digital agency may be proficient at designing communications and interactive marketing experiences, but that does not mean that it has the requisite experience to develop a digital product or service. The steps we outlined earlier should help business buyers understand the differences between the capabilities of service providers, but the best filter is having a good brief and listening to the prospective partner react to it.

Purchase

In many situations, the actual structure of the engagement, how it is going to be arranged financially, is left until the very end. This can arise from the nature of the dance that happens between buyer and seller; no one wants money to "get in the way" of a perfect relationship, but the realities of "How much can I get?" versus "How much can I make?" are rarely too deep below the surface, especially during a first cycle of collaboration. What people don't realize is that price is not the only factor that affects the outcome; the way you structure the relationship does as well.

There will always be big and small projects, first-time relationships and long-standing partnerships, risks driven by need and inspiration, and the need for working in less than ideal circumstances. There is no perfect way to approach the financial arrangement, because it will always be context-sensitive. But there are some pros and cons to the ways that business and design can engage and some different approaches that might make more sense if both sides understand how experience design works.

Agency of Record Models

The agency of record (AOR) model is very attractive to both sides. For buyers, it represents a level of assurance and confidence that they don't have to keep looking for partners. For sellers, an AOR model means predictable recurring revenue, which always makes life easier. AOR models have some of the same dynamics of marriage, one of which is "you can be right, or you can be happy." In a service-based relationship, this is the institutionalization of the principal-agent problem.

The flip side to this, of course, is that the better business and design understand each other, the better the working relationship is, and theoretically, the more efficient the design partner is in creating value and helping the business make the right decisions. But much of this depends on how the business frames problems and how it relies on the relationship. Using an AOR model to solve all problems at the last minute is unlikely to foster a situation in which a design partner can proactively look out for the client's best interests.

One remedy for this that allows for the benefits of the AOR model without the inefficiencies is building long-term relationships with key partners and working with them in more no-bid or noncompetitive circumstances. This can result in a higher degree of trust and value in the relationship. It's also important that it be clear that the business is going to work with a variety of vendors based on need. But it should also be realized that keeping different design partners informed about what role they are playing in helping the business and encouraging discussions among partners can also aid in overall collaboration.

If business is able to bring design partners to the table centered on an experience design view of the business, customers, Brand, and objectives, it can help design partners add more value in the areas where they are most skilled and experienced.

Fixed-Fee Models

Having both buyer and seller agree and be comfortable with a price is always a great approach. But business in general operates of the basis of asymmetrical information. The problems that can arise are the size of the asymmetries, the nature of the information, the risks involved when expectations aren't met, and the amount of money in question.

The main benefit of a fixed-fee approach is the predictability of the pricing and the outcome. When you know exactly what you are going to get and the price doesn't change, things are good. The trick here for business and design is in managing the expectations of what will be delivered.

Many of the points we made about the role of the brief are important with regard to managing expectations and scope—the two main areas that come into question with a fixed-fee arrangement. We strongly urge both business and design to not make too many assumptions and to spend time going through the brief in detail, either before finalizing a contract or before proceeding too far down the collaboration path. It's better to surface uneven expectations before too much time or money has been burned.

Fixed-fee models have been the staple of the design business for many years. For many design projects, where the process and the deliverables (the nouns or artifacts needed in the customer journey) are industry standard, it is quite safe. Within an adequate fixed scope, design can excel in creating great work. This might be specific implementations of artifacts, or it could be design systems that are references for other teams, where the systems define, through example, what a customer experience should be like. Where the fixed-fee approach begins to become a limitation (assuming that both sides will be diligent about setting expectations correctly at the outset) is when an experience design approach is being taken or when the business is hoping to uncover new insights and opportunities. In these cases, information may change along the way, which can affect project objectives.

Other problems with the fixed-fee approach exist. Necessary artifacts might not get considered during the scoping process. As a result, the scope precludes developing sufficient levels of detail needed for these or for each stage of the customer journey. Overall business objectives can change so that a reference design no longer matches the priorities of development (for example, a product or service feature is now no longer included, but it is a mainstay of the work the designer provided). In these cases, businesses may expect that design will revise their work to meet these additional needs, whereas design may feel that they are beyond the scope of the original agreement. This is why we recommend considering time horizons as part of the objectives in the brief. It is much easier to identify these risks and agree on how they will be approached should they arise before they become problems.

Most modern service agreements we see give the buyer the advantage in a fixed-fee model, with the provider shouldering most of the risk. This is because these agreements often give the buyer the right to refuse to accept the outcome, in which case payment isn't required until the provider has satisfied the situation. This means that in fixed-fee engagements, the principal-agent problem and the Elusive Design syndrome are both risks.

If a project can be extremely well scoped, there is a solid brief that everyone understands, and there are clear mechanisms for change management, fixed fees can work. Without these, they may not only jeopardize the working relationship but also become problems that make it into the customer experience. This is why with experience design, we suggest that business think through the implications of a fixed-fee arrangement before assuming that it is the best approach.

Time and Materials Models

Many service relationships are based on time and materials—the buyer pays a prenegotiated hourly rate and is responsible for any materials the service provider needs to buy or use that would not be included in this hourly rate. This arrangement has several advantages. The first is that it can be relatively easy for a buyer to compare skills and costs across providers in order to decide what is the best way to achieve a goal with a given budget window. Another is that it provides flexibility to both sides, because changes in what needs to get done simply require spending a different amount of time, meaning contracts do not have to be renegotiated.

The time and materials model shifts much of the risks to buyers, because they are not guaranteed to get what they want at a specific price. These risks can be compounded when the buyer is not extremely familiar with the process involved and may not know whether the problem is truly more complex than anticipated or if the provider is being inefficient. In some situations these issues are also difficult to identify early on and tend to surface only at critical points, such as delivery dates or the end of budgets.

The other challenge to a time and materials approach that is endemic to technology design and development is that often one can't be sure that something works until after it has been fully tested. The right test procedures and contexts can be complicated, and what may appear to work in one circumstance may fail in another. Although many programs and projects include testing as part of the services, it may be unclear whether a problem resulted from a lack of quality, an unforeseen complexity, or an error in the requirements and expectations of the program or project. The impact may significantly affect costs and timing, but more important, it may go undetected until experienced by a customer.

Many design and development methodologies that are based on a time and materials model have built-in ways of managing priorities and ensuring quality. Trouble can still arise when expectations are not set and managed correctly. Buyers need to be fully aware that a time and materials model does not guarantee that an a priori model is what will be delivered. They also need to understand that the flexibility of the process does not mean that drastic changes to scope can be made at any point. There are still the realities of time already spent that must be paid for and the interdependencies that arise when asking for change (requests for seemingly simple changes can actually be quite substantial to fulfill).

Buyers and providers should agree on how to track progress and budgets to prevent any surprises. One approach is to use estimated caps for specific stages of work. Before engaging, the provider can set up an estimate that will have a sliding scale of precision. The closer in time to a stage, the more precise the estimate (assuming the brief and available information are adequate), while later stages are dependent on progress and changes in earlier stages. Before another stage kicks off, a revised estimate can be created. This allows for discussions about reprioritizing efforts and can help the buyer understand trade-offs from a cost/benefit perspective.

A time and materials approach can be very useful because it alleviates or prevents the principal-agent problem and makes the practice of the Illusive Design syndrome too expensive to be likely It does shift more of the risk to the buyer, but it brings a lot of flexibility to both sides. We like the benefits that this provides and often suggest time and material approaches to programs and projects for experience design.

There is one danger that this approach can create that can seriously undermine a business's efforts to take an experience design approach to creating value: When changes are made midstream, it's often done with the goal of meeting an objective that is important to business stakeholders. However, this may not serve the needs of the customer. The time and materials model can keep both the business buyer and the design service provider happy with their relationship but allow the customer to suffer through poorly designed products and services. When changes are not prioritized based on value for both the business and the end customer, it puts the Brand at risk. When time to market and costs are drivers for decisions, these kinds of mistakes are frequently made.

Many businesses refuse to enter into time and materials relationships because it is difficult to manage costs and be sure of outcomes. But the reality is that if there is not enough information to adequately frame a problem, any other approach is going to introduce the same level of risk, if not more. In addition, most fixed-fee budgets are actually derived through using time and materials estimates anyway. We suggest that businesses be more agreeable to pursuing hybrid relationships, where a time and materials model is used in conjunction with a fixed-fee arrangement, depending on the nature of the problem and the order that components are solved. In our experience this is the best way to ensure that an experience design approach can be used to the fullest advantage for the business and its customers.

Consulting Retainers

We recommend that businesses begin to consider a new form of relationship with design service providers. If you consider how we have presented experience design, you can come to the conclusion that design should be at many more conversations at much earlier stages than is currently occurring. This doesn't mean that projects should be starting earlier, but it may make sense for business to seek input from design at earlier planning stages, even when discussing strategy or significant changes to the business model, products, services, or customer experience.

In this kind of scenario, trusted design partners might provide perspectives that are based on subject matter expertise, or they may simply play the role that in-house design would play if they existed. The benefit would be that a lot of the value that design offers would be accessed when it is needed most: when commitments to objectives are being made.

In this kind of relationship, either a small monthly retainer or a capped but open purchase order could be used and time billed as it is used, with a rollover for unused time.

This kind of relationship would make transitioning to an experience design–centric approach to the world smoother for business and help coordinate the engagement and efforts of other design service providers.

Performance-Based Pay

There are several variations of this kind of relationship, from equity exchanged for services, convertible debt instruments, revenue shares, and rights to license IP. Most design service providers are not venture capitalists and have very different business models, so business should not necessarily expect that all approaches will make sense to every potential partner. But we think there are interesting opportunities to explore, especially in relationships in which the opportunity is interesting but may be too risky for businesses to be able to completely foot the bill on their own.

Design providers also can stumble upon great innovations, largely because of the breadth of industries, businesses, customers, and trends they encounter. These are rarely going to be introduced during a fixed-fee or time and materials engagement, either because the value is much higher than the fees or because the buyer doesn't have the authority to act or doesn't understand the implications. We think it makes sense for strong business-design partners to discuss these kinds of options.

We also strongly advise businesses to start applying some of these models to anyone promising innovation in exchange for huge fees. Too often, these innovations cannot be implemented as defined or can be identified in a more nimble and cost-efficient way. (We recommend that businesses start demanding rebates for significant portions of innovation fees if the innovation proves to be impossible to execute within the given constraints of the context for which it is intended.)

Our experience in watching business and design collaborate has led us to propose the experience design model, but it has also taught us the importance of the initial conditions in determining the outcome of any situation. We think that too often the relationship structure is seen as a mere formality and won't influence or impact the design (and eventually the products, services, and experience customers have with a Brand). We think this is an oversight that can be easily corrected and that businesses that understand and adopt experience design will realize this as well.

Final Thoughts

Our goals in writing this book are not simply to illustrate the thinking, frameworks, and tools of experience design but also to help people put these ideas into action. We are constantly exposed to situations in which substantial efforts need to be applied to help businesses overcome challenges that could have been avoided. We routinely see requests for proposals seeking to improve experiences that are fundamentally flawed because of decisions that were made without thinking about how they would impact customers' perception of value and engagement.

Although it's not possible to provide a single methodology that allows experience design to be used to prevent problems or applied as a point solution to existing problems that can arise from shortsighted decision-making processes, we do want to help readers find ways to adopt an experience design approach for their own roles with their businesses. We believe that understanding the principles of experience design, being able to explain them to others, and helping teams use them to frame and solve problems will do a lot to help business and design more successfully collaborate. We also believe that the ultimate beneficiaries of this will be the customer and the businesses that use the thinking presented here to engage the customer in valuable experiences.

Although we believe that the current ways in which business collaborates with design to produce value for customers are broken and inefficient, we aren't trying to paint a picture that businesses that do not adopt experience design will fail. Nor would we say that adopting the approach to experience design that we have provided here is the only way to do it. Many companies—Disney, Apple, Zappos, Amazon, Target, and many, many more—have been successful simply by figuring out how to deliver the right value through products, services, solutions, and overall experience that meet their customers' needs. They may agree with many of the principles, but we would be very surprised to hear any of them say that they based their strategies on experience design (largely because we haven't heard people use the term *experience design* in this way, and this whole view is emerging and evolving in real time).

What we do believe is that when you think about designing for experiences that provide value and engage customers, you need to have a different perspective. You need to think about how your goals affect your customer's goals and vice versa, and you need to think about how all your efforts—across the entire business—are interrelated. You need to think about how all the experiences your customers have had with you may change the way they think about your Brand, what they expect from you, and how this may be different from what you would normally conclude. You have to think about all of these things, across time frames that are probably broader, and perhaps more integrated and interdependent, than you might normally consider. In addition, you need to think about the larger context in which both your business and your customers exist and take into account how it is affecting the things you are doing and what your customer may expect or want.

We also believe that however you approach the situation, you need to involve design at a strategic level—people familiar with the processes involved who understand what constitutes craftsmanship and who can help plan for successful delivery. Design should be included in early conversations, before you decide what design should do. Design should be invited to the table when you are defining business objectives and deciding how you plan to meet them to help ensure that you have answers to why your approach will be valuable to customers.

We also believe that design needs to arrive at the table with a multidisciplinary perspective and the ability to advise on how design—the process and the outcomes— can be used with the goal of delivering value for customers and creating experiences that keep customers engaged. Design needs to be willing and to understand how and why to make trade-offs that help create success given the real-world constraints that face business. Design cannot have the ivory-tower principles often associated with formal systems of design. Design must revive the maker/designer attitude while applying as much of the excellence of the formal systems as can be permitted by the situation.

UNIVERSITY
LIBRARY

It is also apparent to us that much of the thinking we have laid out here, in principle, may have corollaries and parallels to how businesses structure their operations and think about their ongoing activities.

Strategic consulting is a relatively nascent practice when considered against the overall timeline of commercial activity. We think that this field of thinking is likely to develop overlaps with how we are positioning experience design.

Business process optimization and efficiency planning have focused on driving down costs while improving quality. At some point, there is a logical extension of this into service design and experience planning. There is certainly a benefit to extending the concept of customer beyond the market to also include employees and shareholders. Decisions that always weigh value for all three customers would certainly change the way that businesses view the world. Think about how this might redefine what your Brand's relationship with customers really could mean.

We think the time is right for exploring a tighter integration between business and design. We also think that technology will allow for many new ways of creating and delivering value to customers and engaging with them over time. The prospect of what the future will look like is exciting to us. We are proposing experience design as much for this future as we are to share what we have learned from the past.

We hope that we have set some wheels in motion. We hope that we have clarified some things it terms of what design can do for business. We hope that we have inspired people to look deeper at how they approach Brand and customer experience and why it is important. We also look forward to the discussions that will come from this, but more important to what business and design will create as they really start hitting their stride in collaborating.

Notes

Section I

1   As quoted by Frank Wilson, *The Hand: How Its Use Shapes the Brain, Language, and Human Culture* (New York: Vintage Books, 1999), Kindle edition.

Chapter 1

1   The Firesign Theatre, *Everything You Know Is Wrong* (Columbia KC-33141, October 1974).

2   Samuel Arbesman, *The Half-Life of Facts: Why Everything We Know Has an Expiration Date* (New York: Current, 2012), Kindle edition.

3   Kjetil Fallan, *Design History: Understanding Theory and Method* (Oxford: Berg, 2010), Kindle edition.

4   Matthew B. Crawford, *Shop Class as Soulcraft: An Inquiry into the Value of Work* (New York: Penguin Press, 2009), Kindle edition.

5   Hazel Conway, ed., *Design History: A Student's Handbook* (London: Routledge, 2001), Kindle edition.

6   Frank Wilson, *The Hand: How Its Use Shapes the Brain, Language, and Human Culture* (New York: Vintage Books, 1999), Kindle edition.

7   Lewis Wolpert, *Six Impossible Things before Breakfast: The Evolutionary Origins of Belief* (New York: Norton, 2007).

8   Wilson, *The Hand*.

9   Nassim Nicholas Taleb, *Antifragile: Things That Gain from Disorder* (New York: Random House, 2012), Kindle edition.

10   Crawford, *Shop Class as Soulcraft*.

11   Fallan, *Design History*.

12   Conway, *Design History*.

13   Peter Hutchinson, *A Publisher's History of American Magazines—Magazine Growth in the Nineteenth Century*, 2008, http://themagazinist.com/uploads/Introduction.pdf.

14   Crawford, *Shop Class as Soulcraft*.

15   James B. Twitchell, *Adcult USA: The Triumph of Advertising in American Culture* (New York: Columbia University Press, 1996).

16   Conway, *Design History*.

17   Arbesman, *The Half-Life of Facts*.

18   Chris Anderson, *Makers: The New Industrial Revolution* (New York: Random House Digital, 2012), Kindle edition.

Chapter 2

1   http://en.wikiquote.org/wiki/John_Maynard_Keynes.

2   John Maynard Keynes, *The General Theory of Employment, Interest and Money* (Orlando: First Harvest/Harcourt, 1964).

3   Arthur Schopenhauer, *The Art of Always Being Right: 30 Ways to Win an Argument*, Kindle edition.

4   Howard Gardner, *Frames of Mind: The Theory of Multiple Intelligences* (New York: Basic Books, 2011), Kindle edition.

5   An article on the failure of Porter's Monitor Group describes various critics of Porter's theories: http://www.forbes.com/sites/stevedenning/2012/11/20/what-killed-michael-porters-monitor-group-the-one-force-that-really-matters/.

6   Michael E. Porter and others, *HBR's 10 Must Reads on Strategy (with featured article "What Is Strategy?" by Michael E. Porter)* (Boston: Harvard Business Press Books, 2011), Kindle edition.

7   Ron Adner, *The Wide Lens: A New Strategy for Innovation* (New York: Portfolio/Penguin, 2012), Kindle edition.

8   Ibid.

9   Ibid.

10 Youngme Moon, *Different: Escaping the Competitive Herd* (New York: Crown Business, 2010), Kindle edition.

11 An anecdote told to one of the authors while working with Ernst & Young.

12 Frank Wilson, *The Hand: How Its Use Shapes the Brain, Language, and Human Culture* (New York: Vintage, 1999), Kindle edition.

Chapter 3

1   Stephen Jay Gould, *Time's Arrow, Time's Cycle: Myth and Metaphor in the Discovery of Geological Time* (Boston: Harvard University Press, 1987).

2   Youngme Moon, *Different: Escaping the Competitive Herd* (New York: Crown Business, 2010), Kindle edition.

3   Scott Berkun, *The Myths of Innovation* (Sebastopol: O'Reilly, 2010), Kindle edition.

4   Ron Adner, *The Wide Lens: A New Strategy for Innovation* (New York: Portfolio/Penguin, 2012), Kindle edition.

5   Michael Mainelli and Ian Harris, *The Price of Fish: A New Approach to Wicked Economics and Better Decisions* (London: Nicholas Brealey Publishing, 2011), Kindle edition.

6   Adner, *The Wide Lens*.

7   Mainelli and Harris, *The Price of Fish*.

8   Clayton M. Christensen, Scott D. Anthony, and Erik A. Roth, *Seeing What's Next: Using Theories of Innovation to Predict Industry Change* (Boston: Harvard Business School Publishing, 2004), Kindle edition.

9   http://www.searchquotes.com/quotation/Innovation_is_not_the_product_of_logical_thought,_although_the_result_is_tied_to_logical_structure./228996/.

10 Sims excerpt from the U.S. Army's field manual FM 5–0: Operations Process, Chapter 3, as quoted in Peter Sims, *Little Bets: How Breakthrough Ideas Emerge for Small Discoveries* (New York: Free Press, 2011), Kindle edition.

11 Jeff Dyer, Hal Gregersen, and Clayton Christensen, *The Innovator's DNA* (Boston: Harvard Business Review Press, 2001), Kindle edition.

12 Sims, *Little Bets*.

13 Nassim Nicholas Taleb, *Antifragile: Things That Gain from Disorder* (New York: Random House, 2012), Kindle edition.

Chapter 4

1   As quoted in Michael Mainelli and Ian Harris, *The Price of Fish: A New Approach to Wicked Economics and Better Decisions* (London: Nicholas Brealey Publishing, 2011), Kindle edition.

2   Mainelli and Harris, *The Price of Fish*.

3   Daniel Kahneman, *Thinking, Fast and Slow* (New York: Farrar, Straus and Giroux, 2011), Kindle edition.

4   David Rock, *Your Brain at Work: Strategies for Overcoming Distraction, Regaining Focus, & Working Smarter All Day Long* (New York: HarperCollins, 2009), Kindle edition.

5   Bruce D. Temkin, *The State of Customer Experience*, 2010, Forrester, February 19,
    2010 (http://www.forrester.com/The+State+Of+Customer+Experience+2010/fulltext/-/E
    -RES56316?objectid=RES56316).

6   Howard Gardner, *Frames of Mind: The Theory of Multiple Intelligences* (New York: Basic Books, 2011),
    Kindle edition.

7   B. Joseph Pine II and James H. Gilmore, *The Experience Economy: Work Is Theater & Every Business
    a Stage* (Boston: Harvard Business Press, 1999).

8   Jeff Dyer, Hal Gregersen, and Clayton Christensen, *The Innovator's DNA* (Boston: Harvard Business
    Review Press, 2001), Kindle edition.

Section II

1   http://www.quotationspage.com/quote/2279.html.

Chapter 5

1   As quoted on http://www.allaboutbranding.com/index.lasso?article=22.

2   Kevin Lane Keller, *Strategic Brand Management*, 3rd ed. (Upper Saddle River, NJ: Prentice Hall, 2007).

3   David Aaker, *Building Strong Brands* (New York: Free Press, 1995).

Chapter 6

1   Eric Siegel, *Predictive Analytics: The Power to Predict Who Will Click, Buy, Lie, or Die* (Hoboken, NJ:
    John Wiley & Sons, 2013), Kindle edition.

2   Daniel Kahneman, *Thinking, Fast and Slow* (New York: Farrar, Straus and Giroux, 2011), Kindle edition.

3   Samuel Arbesman, *The Half-Life of Facts: Why Everything We Know Has an Expiration Date* (New York:
    Current, 2012), Kindle edition.

4   Ron Adner, *The Wide Lens: A New Strategy for Innovation* (New York: Portfolio/Penguin, 2012), Kindle
    edition.

Section III

1   http://www.searchquotes.com/quotation/Perfection_of_means_and_confusion_of_ends_seem_to_
    characterize_our_age./5697/.

2   Kathryn Schulz, *Being Wrong: Adventures in the Margin of Error* (New York: Ecco Press, 2011).

Chapter 9

1   Youngme Moon, *Different: Escaping the Competitive Herd* (New York: Crown Business, 2010), Kindle
    edition.

Acknowledgments

This book is largely a product of the experiences we have had as a company over the past 15 years. During this time we have had the great fortune to work with some extremely smart and talented people—Method employees and Method clients.

We would like to thank all of those people who have worked at Method over the years. Your curiosity, skills, enthusiasm, and belief have helped create a significant body of work. Your thinking has helped us form and articulate what we feel is a foundational toolset that we can all use moving forward—the view of experience design we put forth in this book.

We would also like to thank all of the clients who have worked with us over the years. We have learned a lot about how business sees design, as well as the challenges and opportunities that businesses face in serving markets, shareholders, and employees. Your confidence in us and willingness to collaborate has helped push our potential and has helped us to develop experience design as a new way for design and business to collaborate.

Index

UNIVERSITY OF WINCHESTER
LIBRARY